Middle Ages
Ages
Biographies

Middle Ages Biographies

Volume 2:
J-Z

JUDSON KNIGHT
Edited by Judy Galens

AN IMPRINT OF THE GALE GROUP

DETROIT · NEW YORK · SAN FRANCISCO
LONDON · BOSTON · WOODBRIDGE, CT

Judson Knight

Judy Galens, *Editor*

Staff

Diane Sawinski, *U•X•L Senior Editor*
Carol DeKane Nagel, *U•X•L Managing Editor*
Thomas L. Romig, *U•X•L Publisher*

Margaret Chamberlain, *Permissions Associate (Pictures)*
Maria Franklin, *Permissions Manager*

Randy Bassett, *Imaging Database Supervisor*
Daniel Newell, *Imaging Specialist*
Pamela A. Reed, *Image Coordinator*
Robyn V. Young, *Senior Image Editor*

Rita Wimberley, *Senior Buyer*
Evi Seoud, *Assistant Production Manager*
Dorothy Maki, *Manufacturing Manager*

Pamela A. E. Galbreath, *Senior Art Director*
Kenn Zorn, *Product Design Manager*

Marco Di Vita, the Graphix Group, *Typesetting*

Cover photograph of T'ai Tsung reproduced by permission of the Granger Collection, New York.

Library of Congress Card Number: 00-064864

ISBN 0-7876-4857-4 (set)
ISBN 0-7876-4858-2 (vol. 1)
ISBN 0-7876-4859-0 (vol. 2)

Printed in the United States of America
10 9 8 7 6 5 4 3 2 1

Contents

Volume 1 (A–I)

Volume 2 (J–Z)

Reader's Guide

The Middle Ages was an era of great changes in civilization, a transition between ancient times and the modern world. Lasting roughly from A.D. 500 to 1500, the period saw the growth of the Roman Catholic Church in Western Europe and the spread of the Islamic faith in the Middle East. Around the world, empires—the Byzantine, Mongol, and Incan—rose and fell, and the first nation-states emerged in France, England, and Spain. Despite the beauty of illuminated manuscripts, soaring Gothic cathedrals, and the literary classics of Augustine and Dante, Europe's civilization lagged far behind that of the technologically advanced, administratively organized, and economically wealthy realms of the Arab world, West Africa, India, and China.

Middle Ages: Biographies (two volumes) presents the life stories of fifty people who lived during the Middle Ages. Included are such major rulers as Charlemagne, Genghis Khan, and Eleanor of Aquitaine; thinkers and writers Augustine and Thomas Aquinas; religious leaders Muhammad and Francis of Assisi; and great explorers Marco Polo and Leif Eriksson. Also featured are lesser-known figures from the era, including Wu Ze-tian and Irene of Athens, the only female rulers in the history of China and Byzantium, respectively; Mansa Musa, leader of the great empire of Mali in Africa; Japanese woman author Murasaki Shikibu, who penned the world's first novel; and Pachacutec, Inca emperor recognized as among the greatest rulers in history.

Additional features

Over one hundred illustrations and dozens of sidebar boxes exploring high-interest people and topics bring the text to life. Definitions of unfamiliar terms and a list of books and Web sites to consult for more information are included in each entry. The volume also contains a timeline of events, a general glossary, and an index offering easy access to the people, places, and subjects discussed throughout *Middle Ages: Biographies.*

Dedication

To Margaret, my mother; to Deidre, my wife; and to Tyler, my daughter.

Comments and suggestions

We welcome your comments on this work as well as your suggestions for topics to be featured in future editions of *Middle Ages: Biographies.* Please write: Editors, *Middle Ages: Biographies,* U•X•L, 27500 Drake Rd., Farmington Hills, MI 48331-3535; call toll-free: 1-800-877-4253; fax: 248-699-8097; or send e-mail via www.galegroup.com.

Timeline of Events in the Middle Ages

180   The death of Roman emperor Marcus Aurelius marks the end of the "Pax Romana," or Roman peace. Years of instability follow, and although Rome recovers numerous times, this is the beginning of Rome's three-century decline.

312   Roman emperor Constantine converts to Christianity. As a result, the empire that once persecuted Christians will embrace their religion and eventually will begin to persecute other religions.

325   Constantine calls the Council of Nicaea, first of many ecumenical councils at which gatherings of bishops determine official church policy.

330   Constantine establishes Byzantium as eastern capital of the Roman Empire.

395   After the death of Emperor Theodosius, the Roman Empire is permanently divided in half. As time passes, the Eastern Roman Empire (later known as the Byzantine Empire) distances itself from the declining Western Roman Empire.

410 Led by Alaric, the Visigoths sack Rome, dealing the Western Roman Empire a blow from which it will never recover.

413–425 Deeply affected—as are most Roman citizens—by the Visigoths' attack on Rome, **Augustine** writes *City of God,* one of the most important books of the Middle Ages.

455 The Vandals sack Rome.

c. 459 Death of **St. Patrick**, missionary who converted Ireland to Christianity.

476 The German leader Odoacer removes Emperor Romulus Augustulus and crowns himself "king of Italy." This incident marks the end of the Western Roman Empire.

481 The Merovingian Age, named for the only powerful dynasty in Western Europe during the period, begins when **Clovis** takes the throne in France.

496 **Clovis** converts to Christianity. By establishing strong ties with the pope, he forges a strong church-state relationship that will continue throughout the medieval period.

500 Date commonly cited as beginning of Middle Ages.

500–1000 Era in European history often referred to as the Dark Ages, or Early Middle Ages.

524 The philosopher **Boethius**, from the last generation of classically educated Romans, dies in jail, probably at the orders of the Ostrogoth chieftain Theodoric.

529 Benedict of Nursia and his followers establish the monastery at Monte Cassino, Italy. This marks the beginning of the monastic tradition in Europe.

532 Thanks in large part to the counsel of his wife Theodora, **Justinian**—greatest of Byzantine emperors—takes a strong stand in the Nika Revolt, ensuring his continued power.

534–563 Belisarius and other generals under orders from **Justinian** recapture much of the Western Roman Empire, including parts of Italy, Spain, and North Africa. The victories are costly, however, and soon after Justinian's death these lands will fall back into the hands of barbarian tribes such as the Vandals and Lombards.

535   **Justinian** establishes his legal code, a model for the laws in many Western nations today.

540   The Huns, or Hunas, destroy India's Gupta Empire, plunging much of the subcontinent into a state of anarchy.

c. 550 Death of Indian mathematician **Aryabhata**, one of the first mathematicians to use the numeral zero.

589   The ruthless **Wen Ti** places all of China under the rule of his Sui dynasty, ending more than three centuries of upheaval.

590   Pope **Gregory I** begins his fourteen-year reign. Also known as Gregory the Great, he ensures the survival of the church, and becomes one of its greatest medieval leaders.

Late 500s The first Turks begin moving westward, toward the Middle East, from their homeland to the north and west of China.

604   Prince **Shotoku Taishi** of Japan issues his "Seventeen-Article Constitution."

c. 610 An Arab merchant named **Muhammad** receives the first of some 650 revelations that form the basis of the Koran, Islam's holy book.

618   In China, **T'ai Tsung** and his father Kao Tsu overthrow the cruel Sui dynasty, establishing the highly powerful and efficient T'ang dynasty.

622   **Muhammad** and his followers escape the city of Mecca. This event, known as the *hegira,* marks the beginning of the Muslim calendar.

632–661 Following the death of **Muhammad**, the Arab Muslims are led by a series of four caliphs who greatly expand Muslim territories to include most of the Middle East.

645   A conspiracy to murder the Japanese emperor places the reform-minded Emperor Tenchi on the throne and puts the Fujiwara clan—destined to remain influential for centuries—in a position of power.

661	The fifth caliph, Mu'awiya, founds the Umayyad caliphate, which will rule the Muslim world from Damascus, Syria, until 750.
690	**Wu Ze-tian** becomes sole empress of China. She will reign until 705, the only female ruler in four thousand years of Chinese history.
711	Moors from North Africa invade Spain, taking over from the Visigoths. Muslims will rule parts of the Iberian Peninsula until 1492.
711	Arabs invade the Sind in western India, establishing a Muslim foothold on the Indian subcontinent.
727	In Greece, the Iconoclasts begin a sixty-year war on icons, or images of saints and other religious figures, which they consider idols. Though the Greek Orthodox Church ultimately rejects iconoclasm, the controversy helps widen a growing division between Eastern and Western Christianity.
731	**The Venerable Bede** publishes his *Ecclesiastical History of the English People,* his most important work.
732	A force led by Charles Martel repels Moorish invaders at Tours, halting Islam's advance into Western Europe.
750	A descendant of **Muhammad**'s uncle Abbas begins killing off all the Umayyad leaders and establishes the Abbasid caliphate in Baghdad, Iraq.
751	The Carolingian Age begins when Charles Martel's son Pepin III, with the support of the pope, removes the last Merovingian king from power.
751	Defeated by Arab armies at Talas, China's T'ang dynasty begins to decline. A revolt led by An Lu-shan in 755 adds to its troubles.
768	Reign of **Charlemagne**, greatest ruler of Western Europe during the Early Middle Ages, begins.
782	English scholar **Alcuin** goes to France, on the invitation of **Charlemagne**, to organize a school for future officials in the Carolingian empire.
787	**Irene of Athens** convenes the Seventh Council of Nicaea, which restores the use of icons in worship.

793   Viking raiders destroy the church at Lindisfarne off the coast of England. Lindisfarne was one of the places where civilized learning had weathered the darkest years of the Middle Ages. Thus begins two centuries of terror as more invaders pour out of Scandinavia and spread throughout Europe.

797   Having murdered her son, **Irene of Athens**—who actually ruled from 780 onward—officially becomes Byzantine empress, the only woman ruler in the empire's eleven-hundred-year history. It is partly in reaction to Irene that the pope later crowns **Charlemagne** emperor of Western Europe.

800s   Feudalism takes shape in Western Europe.

800   Pope Leo III crowns **Charlemagne** "Emperor of All the Romans." This marks the beginning of the political alliance later to take shape under **Otto the Great** as the Holy Roman Empire.

c. 800   The Khmers, or Cambodians, adopt Hinduism under the leadership of their first powerful king, Jayavarman II, founder of the Angkor Empire.

801   Death of **Rabia al-Adawiyya**, a woman and former slave who founded the mystic Sufi sect of Islam.

820   A group of Vikings settles in northwestern France, where they will become known as Normans.

843   In the Treaty of Verdun, **Charlemagne**'s son Louis the Pious divides the Carolingian Empire among his three sons. These three parts come to be known as the West Frankish Empire, consisting chiefly of modern France; the "Middle Kingdom," a strip running from what is now the Netherlands all the way down to Italy; and the East Frankish Empire, or modern Germany. The Middle Kingdom soon dissolves into a patchwork of tiny principalities.

c. 850   Death of Arab mathematician **al-Khwarizmi**, who coined the term "algebra" and who is often considered the greatest mathematician of the Middle Ages.

860   Vikings discover Iceland.

863	**St. Cyril** and **St. Methodius**, two Greek priests, become missionaries to the Slavs of Central and Eastern Europe. As a result, the Greek Orthodox version of Christianity spreads throughout the region, along with the Cyrillic alphabet, which the brothers create in order to translate the Bible into local languages.
886	King Alfred the Great captures London from the Danes, and for the first time in British history unites all Anglo-Saxons.
907	China's T'ang dynasty comes to an end after almost three centuries of rule, and the empire enters a period of instability known as "Five Dynasties and Ten Kingdoms."
911	The last of the Carolingian line in the East Frankish Empire dies. Seven years later, Henry the Fowler of Saxony, father of **Otto the Great**, takes leadership of the German states.
c. 930	Arab physician **al-Razi** writes his most important work, *The Comprehensive Book,* which sums up the medical knowledge of the era.
955	German king Otto I defeats a tribe of nomadic invaders called the Magyars. The Magyars later become Christianized and found the nation of Hungary; as for Otto, thenceforth he is known as **Otto the Great.**
957	Death of **al-Mas'udi**, perhaps the greatest historian of the Arab world.
960	In China, troops loyal to Chao K'uang-yin declare him emperor, initiating the Sung dynasty.
962	Having conquered most of Central Europe, **Otto the Great** is crowned emperor in Rome, reviving Charlemagne's title. From this point on, most German kings are also crowned ruler of the Holy Roman Empire.
982	Vikings discover Greenland. Four years later, Erik the Red founds a permanent settlement there.
987	Russia converts to Greek Orthodox Christianity and gradually begins adopting Byzantine culture after Vladimir the Great marries Anne, sister of Emperor **Basil II.**

987   The last Carolingian ruler of France dies without an heir, and Hugh Capet takes the throne, establishing a dynasty that will last until 1328.

1000–1300   Era in European history often referred to as the High Middle Ages.

1001   Vikings led by **Leif Eriksson** sail westward to North America, and during the next two decades conduct a number of raids on the coast of what is now Canada.

1001   A second Muslim invasion of the Indian subcontinent, this time by Turks, takes place as the Ghaznavids subdue a large region in what is now Afghanistan, Pakistan, and western India.

1002   Holy Roman Emperor **Otto III** dies at the age of twenty-two, and with him die his grand dreams of a revived Roman Empire.

1002   In Japan, **Murasaki Shikibu** begins writing the *Tale of Genji*, the world's first novel.

1014   After years of conflict with the Bulgarians, Byzantine Emperor **Basil II** defeats them. He orders that ninety-nine of every one hundred men be blinded and the last man allowed to keep just one eye so he can lead the others home. Bulgaria's Czar Samuel dies of a heart attack when he sees his men, and Basil earns the nickname "Bulgar-Slayer."

1025   **Basil II** dies, having taken the Byzantine Empire to its greatest height since **Justinian** five centuries earlier; however, it begins a rapid decline soon afterward.

1039   Death of Arab mathematician and physicist **Alhazen**, the first scientist to form an accurate theory of optics, or the mechanics of vision.

1054   After centuries of disagreement over numerous issues, the Greek Orthodox Church and the Roman Catholic Church officially separate.

1060   Five years after Turks seize control of Baghdad from the declining Abbasid caliphate, their leader, Toghril Beg, declares himself sultan and thus establishes the Seljuk dynasty.

1066   **William the Conqueror** leads an invading force that defeats an Anglo-Saxon army at Hastings and wins control of England. The Norman invasion is the most important event of medieval English history, greatly affecting the future of English culture and language.

1071   The Seljuk Turks defeat Byzantine forces at the Battle of Manzikert in Armenia. As a result, the Turks gain a foothold in Asia Minor (today known as Turkey), and the Byzantine Empire begins a long, slow decline.

1071   A Norman warlord named Robert Guiscard drives the last Byzantine forces out of Italy. Byzantium had controlled parts of the peninsula since the time of **Justinian**.

1072   Robert Guiscard's brother Roger expels the Arabs from Sicily, and takes control of the island.

1075–77 Pope **Gregory VII** and Holy Roman Emperor **Henry IV** become embroiled in a church-state struggle called the Investiture Controversy, a debate over whether popes or emperors should have the right to appoint local bishops. Deserted by his supporters, Henry stands barefoot in the snow for three days outside the gates of a castle in Canossa, Italy, waiting to beg the pope's forgiveness.

1084   Reversing the results of an earlier round in the Investiture Controversy, **Henry IV** takes Rome and forcibly removes **Gregory VII** from power. The pope dies soon afterward, broken and humiliated.

1084   **Ssu-ma Kuang**, an official in the Sung dynasty, completes his monumental history of China, *Comprehensive Mirror for Aid in Government*.

1094   Troops under the leadership of Rodrigo Díaz de Vivar—better known as **El Cid**—defeat the Moorish Almoravids at Valencia. This victory, and the character of El Cid himself, becomes a symbol of the Reconquista, the Christian effort to reclaim Spain from its Muslim conquerors.

1094   Norman warrior Bohemond, son of Robert Guiscard, takes control of Rome from **Henry IV** and hands the city over to Pope Urban II. Fearing the Normans' power and aware that he owes them a great debt, Urban looks for something to divert their attention.

1095   Byzantine Emperor Alexis Comnenus asks Urban II for military assistance against the Turks. Urban preaches a sermon to raise support at the Council of Clermont in France, and in the resulting fervor the First Crusade begins. Among its leaders are Bohemond and his nephew Tancred.

1096–97 A pathetic sideshow called the Peasants' Crusade plays out before the real First Crusade gets underway. The peasants begin by robbing and killing thousands of Jews in Germany; then, led by Peter the Hermit, they march toward the Holy Land, wreaking havoc as they go. In Anatolia, a local Turkish sultan leads them into a trap, and most of the peasants are killed.

1099   The First Crusade ends in victory for the Europeans as they conquer Jerusalem. It is a costly victory, however—one in which thousands of innocent Muslims, as well as many Europeans, have been brutally slaughtered—and it sows resentment between Muslims and Christians that remains strong today.

c. 1100–1300 Many of the aspects of life most commonly associated with the Middle Ages, including heraldry and chivalry, make their appearance in Western Europe during this period. Returning crusaders adapt the defensive architecture they observed in fortresses of the Holy Land, resulting in the familiar design of the medieval castle. This is also the era of romantic and heroic tales such as those of King Arthur.

1105   King Henry I of England and St. **Anselm of Canterbury**, head of the English church, sign an agreement settling their differences. This is an important milestone in church-state relations and serves as the model for the Concordat of Worms seventeen years later.

1118   After being banished because of her part in a conspiracy against her brother, the Byzantine emperor, **Anna Comnena** begins writing the *Alexiad*, a history of Byzantium in the period 1069–1118.

1140 After a career in which he infuriated many with his unconventional views on God, French philosopher **Peter Abelard** is charged with heresy by **Bernard of Clairvaux** and forced to publicly refute his beliefs.

c. 1140 In Cambodia, Khmer emperor Suryavarman II develops the splendid temple complex of Angkor Wat.

1146 After the Muslims' capture of Edessa in 1144, Pope Eugenius III calls on the help of his former teacher, **Bernard of Clairvaux**, who makes a speech that leads to the launching of the Second Crusade.

1147–49 In the disastrous Second Crusade, armies from Europe are double-crossed by their crusader allies in the Latin Kingdom of Jerusalem. They fail to recapture Edessa and suffer a heavy defeat at Damascus. Among the people who take part in the crusade (though not as a combatant) is **Eleanor of Aquitaine.**

1154 After the death of England's King Stephen, Henry II takes the throne, beginning the long Plantaganet dynasty. With Henry is his new bride, **Eleanor of Aquitaine.** Now queen of England, she had been queen of France two years earlier, before the annulment of her marriage to King Louis VII.

1158 Holy Roman Emperor **Frederick I Barbarossa** establishes Europe's first university at Bologna, Italy.

1159 **Frederick I Barbarossa** begins a quarter-century of fruitless, costly wars in which the Ghibellines and Guelphs—factions representing pro-imperial and pro-church forces, respectively—fight for control of northern Italy.

1162 **Moses Maimonides,** greatest Jewish philosopher of the Middle Ages, publishes his *Letter Concerning Apostasy,* the first of many important works by him that will appear over the next four decades.

1165 A letter supposedly written by Prester John, a Christian monarch in the East, appears in Europe. Over the centuries that follow, Europeans will search in vain for Prester John, hoping for his aid in their war against Muslim forces. Even as Europe enters the modern era, early proponents of exploration such as

Henry the Navigator will remain inspired by the quest for Prester John's kingdom.

1170   Knights loyal to Henry II murder the archbishop **Thomas à Becket** in his cathedral at Canterbury.

1174–80 Arab philosopher **Averroës** writes one of his most important works, *The Incoherence of the Incoherence,* a response to hard-line Muslim attacks on his belief that reason and religious faith can coexist.

1183   **Frederick I Barbarossa** signs the Peace of Constance with the cities of the Lombard League, and thus ends his long war in northern Italy. After this he will concentrate his attention on Germany and institute reforms that make him a hero in his homeland.

1185   For the first time, Japan comes under the rule of a shogun, or military dictator. Shoguns will remain in power for the next four centuries.

1187   Muslim armies under **Saladin** deal the crusaders a devastating blow at the Battle of Hittin in Palestine. Shortly afterward, Saladin leads his armies in the reconquest of Jerusalem.

1189   In response to **Saladin**'s victories, Europeans launch the Third Crusade. Of the crusade's three principal leaders, Emperor **Frederick I Barbarossa** drowns on his way to the Holy Land, and **Richard I** takes a number of detours, only arriving in 1191. This leaves Philip II Augustus of France to fight the Muslims alone.

1191   Led by **Richard I** of England and Philip II of France, crusaders take the city of Acre in Palestine.

1192   **Richard I** signs a treaty with **Saladin**, ending the Third Crusade.

1198   Pope **Innocent III** begins an eighteen-year reign that marks the high point of the church's power. Despite his great influence, however, when he calls for a new crusade to the Holy Land, he gets little response—a sign that the spirit behind the Crusades is dying.

c. 1200 Cambodia's Khmer Empire reaches its height under Jayavarman VII.

1202 Four years after the initial plea from the pope, the Fourth Crusade begins. Instead of going to the Holy Land, however, the crusaders become involved in a power struggle for the Byzantine throne.

1204 Acting on orders from the powerful city-state of Venice, crusaders take Constantinople, forcing the Byzantines to retreat to Trebizond in Turkey. The Fourth Crusade ends with the establishment of the Latin Empire.

1206 Qutb-ud-Din Aybak, the first independent Muslim ruler in India, establishes the Delhi Sultanate.

1206 **Genghis Khan** unites the Mongols for the first time in their history and soon afterward leads them to war against the Sung dynasty in China.

1208 Pope **Innocent III** launches the Albigensian Crusade against the Cathars, a heretical sect in southern France.

1209 **St. Francis of Assisi** establishes the Franciscan order.

1215 In Rome, Pope **Innocent III** convenes the Fourth Lateran Council. A number of traditions, such as regular confession of sin to a priest, are established at this, one of the most significant ecumenical councils in history.

1215 English noblemen force King John to sign the Magna Carta, which grants much greater power to the nobility. Ultimately the agreement will lead to increased freedom for the people from the power of both king and nobles.

1217–21 In the Fifth Crusade, armies from England, Germany, Hungary, and Austria attempt unsuccessfully to conquer Egypt.

1227 **Genghis Khan** dies, having conquered much of China and Central Asia, thus laying the foundation for the largest empire in history.

1228–29 The Sixth Crusade, led by Holy Roman Emperor **Frederick II**, results in a treaty that briefly restores Christian control of Jerusalem—and does so with a minimum of bloodshed.

1229   The brutal Albigensian Crusade ends. Not only are the Cathars destroyed, but so is much of the French nobility, thus greatly strengthening the power of the French king.

1231   Pope Gregory IX establishes the Inquisition, a court through which the church will investigate, try, and punish cases of heresy.

c. 1235 The empire of Mali, most powerful realm in sub-Saharan Africa at the time, takes shape under the leadership of Sundiata Keita.

1239–40 In the Seventh Crusade, Europeans make another failed attempt to retake the Holy Land.

1241   After six years of campaigns in which they sliced across Russia and Eastern Europe, a Mongol force is poised to take Vienna, Austria, and thus to swarm into Western Europe. But when their leader, Batu Khan, learns that the Great Khan Ogodai is dead, he rushes back to the Mongol capital at Karakorum to participate in choosing a successor.

1242   **Alexander Nevsky** and his brother Andrew lead the Russians' defense of Novgorod against invaders from Germany.

1243   Back on the warpath, but this time in the Middle East, the Mongols defeat the last remnants of the Seljuk Turks.

1248–54 King Louis IX of France (St. Louis) leads the Eighth Crusade, this time against the Mamluks. The result is the same: yet another defeat for the Europeans.

1252   In Egypt, a group of former slave soldiers called the Mamluks take power from the Ayyubid dynasty, established many years before by **Saladin.**

1260   The Mamluks become the first force to defeat the Mongols, in a battle at Goliath Spring in Palestine.

1260   **Kublai Khan**, greatest Mongol leader after his grandfather **Genghis Khan**, is declared Great Khan, or leader of the Mongols.

1261   Led by Michael VIII Palaeologus, the Byzantines recapture Constantinople from the Latin Empire, and

Byzantium enjoys one last gasp of power before it goes into terminal decline.

1270–72 In the Ninth Crusade, last of the numbered crusades, King Louis IX of France again leads the Europeans against the Mamluks, who defeat European forces yet again.

1271 **Marco Polo** embarks on his celebrated journey to the East, which lasts twenty-four years.

1273 The Hapsburg dynasty—destined to remain a major factor in European politics until 1918—takes control of the Holy Roman Empire.

1273 Italian philosopher and theologian **Thomas Aquinas** completes the crowning work of his career, the monumental *Summa theologica*. The influential book will help lead to wider acceptance of the idea, introduced earlier by **Moses Maimonides**, **Averroës**, and **Abelard**, that reason and faith are compatible.

1279 Mongol forces under **Kublai Khan** win final victory over China's Sung dynasty. Thus begins the Yüan dynasty, the first time in Chinese history when the country has been ruled by foreigners.

1291 Mamluks conquer the last Christian stronghold at Acre, bringing to an end two centuries of crusades to conquer the Holy Land for Christendom.

1292 Death of **Roger Bacon**, one of Europe's most important scientists. His work helped to show the rebirth of scientific curiosity taking place in Europe as a result of contact with the Arab world during the Crusades.

1294 At the death of **Kublai Khan**, the Mongol realm is the largest empire in history, covering most of Asia and a large part of Europe. Within less than a century, however, this vast empire will have all but disappeared.

1299 Turkish chieftain **Osman I** refuses to pay tribute to the local Mongol rulers, marking the beginnings of the Ottoman Empire.

1300–1500 Era in European history often referred to as the Late Middle Ages.

1303   After years of conflict with Pope Boniface VIII, France's King Philip the Fair briefly has the pope arrested. This event and its aftermath marks the low point of the papacy during the Middle Ages.

1308   **Dante Alighieri** begins writing the *Divine Comedy*, which he will complete shortly before his death in 1321.

1309   Pope Clement V, an ally of Philip the Fair, moves the papal seat from Rome to Avignon in southern France.

1309   After years of fighting, Sultan **Ala-ud-din Muhammad Khalji** subdues most of India.

1324   **Mansa Musa**, emperor of Mali, embarks on a pilgrimage to Mecca. After stopping in Cairo, Egypt, and spending so much gold that he affects the region's economy for years, he becomes famous throughout the Western world: the first sub-Saharan African ruler widely known among Europeans.

1328   Because of a dispute between the Franciscans and the papacy, **William of Ockham**, one of the late medieval period's most important philosophers, is forced to flee the papal court. He remains under the protection of the Holy Roman emperor for the rest of his life.

1337   England and France begin fighting what will become known as the Hundred Years' War, an on-again, off-again struggle to control parts of France.

1347–51 Europe experiences one of the worst disasters in human history, an epidemic called the Black Death. Sometimes called simply "the Plague," in four years the Black Death kills some thirty-five million people, or approximately one-third of the European population in 1300.

1368   Led by Chu Yüan-chang, a group of rebels overthrows the Mongol Yüan dynasty of China and establishes the Ming dynasty, China's last native-born ruling house.

1378   The Catholic Church becomes embroiled in the Great Schism, which will last until 1417. During this time, there are rival popes in Rome and Avignon; and from 1409 to 1417, there is even a third pope in Pisa, Italy.

1383 **Tamerlane** embarks on two decades of conquest in which he strikes devastating blows against empires in Turkey, Russia, and India and subdues a large portion of central and southwestern Asia.

1386 **Geoffrey Chaucer** begins writing the *Canterbury Tales.*

1389 Ottoman forces defeat the Serbs in battle at Kosovo Field. As a result, all of Southeastern Europe except for Greece falls under Turkish control.

1390 **Tamerlane** attacks and severely weakens the Golden Horde even though its leaders come from the same Mongol and Tatar ancestry as he.

1392 General Yi Song-ye seizes power in Korea and establishes a dynasty that will remain in control until 1910.

1398 **Tamerlane** sacks the Indian city of Delhi, hastening the end of the Delhi Sultanate, which comes in 1413.

1402 After conquering much of Iran and surrounding areas and then moving westward, **Tamerlane** defeats the Ottoman sultan Bajazed in battle. An unexpected result of their defeat is that the Ottomans, who seemed poised to take over much of Europe, go into a period of decline.

1404–05 **Christine de Pisan**, Europe's first female professional writer, publishes *The Book of the City of Ladies,* her most celebrated work.

1405 Ming dynasty emperor Yung-lo sends Admiral Cheng Ho on the first of seven westward voyages. These take place over the next quarter-century, during which time Chinese ships travel as far as East Africa.

1417 The Council of Constance ends the Great Schism, affirming that Rome is the seat of the church and that Pope Martin V is its sole leader. Unfortunately for the church, the Great Schism has weakened it at the very time that it faces its greatest challenge ever: a gathering movement that will come to be known as the Reformation.

1418   The "school" of navigation founded by Prince **Henry the Navigator** sponsors the first of many expeditions that, over the next forty-two years, will greatly increase knowledge of the middle Atlantic Ocean and Africa's west coast. These are the earliest European voyages of exploration, of which there will be many in the next two centuries.

1421   Emperor Yung-lo moves the Chinese capital from Nanjing to Beijing, where it has remained virtually ever since.

1429   A tiny French army led by **Joan of Arc** forces the English to lift their siege on the town of Orléans, a victory that raises French spirits and makes it possible for France's king Charles VII to be crowned later that year. This marks a turning point in the Hundred Years' War.

1430–31 Captured by Burgundian forces, **Joan of Arc** is handed over to the English, who arrange her trial for witchcraft in a court of French priests. The trial, a mockery of justice, ends with Joan being burned at the stake.

1431   In Southeast Asia, the Thais conquer the Angkor Empire.

1431   The Aztecs become the dominant partner in a triple alliance with two nearby city-states and soon afterward gain control of the Valley of Mexico.

1438   **Pachacutec Inca Yupanqui**, greatest Inca ruler, takes the throne.

1440   **Montezuma I** takes the Aztec throne.

1441   Fourteen black slaves are brought from Africa to Portugal, where they are presented to Prince **Henry the Navigator.** This is the beginning of the African slave trade, which isn't abolished until more than four centuries later.

1451	The recovery of the Ottoman Empire, which had suffered a half-century of decline, begins under Mehmet the Conqueror.
1453	Due in large part to the victories of **Joan of Arc**, which lifted French morale twenty-four years earlier, the Hundred Years' War ends with French victory.
1453	Turks under Mehmet the Conqueror march into Constantinople, bringing about the fall of the Byzantine Empire. Greece will remain part of the Ottoman Empire until 1829.
1455	Having developed a method of movable-type printing, Johannes Gutenberg of Mainz, Germany, prints his first book: a Bible. In the years to come, the invention of the printing press will prove to be one of the most important events in world history.
1456	A commission directed by Pope Calixtus III declares that the verdict against **Joan of Arc** in 1431 had been wrongfully obtained.
1470	One of the first printed books to appear in England, *La Morte D'Arthur* by Sir Thomas Malory helps establish the now-familiar tales of Arthurian legend.
1492	Spain, united by the 1469 marriage of its two most powerful monarchs, Ferdinand II of Aragon and Isabella I of Castile, drives out the last of the Muslims and expels all Jews. A less significant event of 1492, from the Spanish perspective, is the launch of a naval expedition in search of a westward sea route to China. Its leader is an Italian sailor named Christopher Columbus, who has grown up heavily influenced by **Marco Polo**'s account of his travels.
1493	**Mohammed I Askia** takes the throne of Africa's Songhai Empire, which will reach its height under his leadership.
1500	Date commonly cited as the end of Middle Ages, and the beginning of the Renaissance.
1517	Exactly a century after the Council of Constance ended the Great Schism, a German monk named Martin Luther publicly posts ninety-five theses, or statements challenging the established teachings of

Catholicism, on the door of a church in Germany. Over the next century, numerous new Protestant religious denominations will be established.

1521   Spanish forces led by the conquistador Hernán Cortés destroy the Aztec Empire.

1526   Babur, a descendant of **Tamerlane**, invades India and establishes what becomes the Mogul Empire.

1533   Francisco Pizarro and the Spanish forces with him arrive in Peru and soon bring about the end of the Inca Empire.

1591   Songhai, the last of the great premodern empires in Africa's Sudan region, falls to invaders from Morocco.

1806   In the process of conquering most of Europe, Napoleon Bonaparte brings the Holy Roman Empire to an end.

1912   More than twenty-one centuries of imperial rule in China end with the overthrow of the government by revolutionary forces, who establish a republic.

1918   Among the many outcomes of World War I are the disintegration of several empires with roots in the Middle Ages: the Austro-Hungarian, Ottoman, and Russian empires.

1960s   Nearly a thousand years after **Leif Eriksson** and other Vikings visited the New World, archaeologists find remains of a Norse settlement in Newfoundland.

Words to Know

A

Age of Exploration: The period from about 1450 to about 1750 when European explorers conducted their most significant voyages and travels around the world.

Alchemy: A semi-scientific discipline that holds that through the application of certain chemical processes, ordinary metals can be turned into gold.

Algebra: A type of mathematics used to determine the value of unknown quantities where these can be related to known numbers.

Allegory: A type of narrative, popular throughout the Middle Ages, in which characters represent ideas.

Anarchy: Breakdown of political order.

Ancestor: An earlier person in one's line of parentage, usually more distant in time than a grandparent.

Anti-Semitism: Hatred of, or discrimination against, Jews.

Antipope: A priest proclaimed pope by one group or another, but not officially recognized by the church.

Archaeology: The scientific study of past civilizations.

Archbishop: The leading bishop in an area or nation.

Aristocracy: The richest and most powerful members of society.

Ascetic: A person who renounces all earthly pleasures as part of his or her search for religious understanding.

Assassination: Killing, usually of an important leader, for political reasons.

Astronomy: The scientific study of the stars and other heavenly bodies and their movement in the sky.

B

Barbarian: A negative term used to describe someone as uncivilized.

Bishop: A figure in the Christian church assigned to oversee priests and believers in a given city or region.

Bureaucracy: A network of officials who run a government.

C

Caliph: A successor to Muhammad as spiritual and political leader of Islam.

Caliphate: The domain ruled by a caliph.

Canonization: Formal declaration of a deceased person as a saint.

Cardinal: An office in the Catholic Church higher than that of bishop or archbishop; the seventy cardinals in the "College of Cardinals" participate in electing the pope.

Cavalry: Soldiers on horseback.

Chivalry: The system of medieval knighthood, particularly its code of honor with regard to women.

Christendom: The Christian world.

Church: The entire Christian church, or more specifically the Roman Catholic Church.

City-state: A city that is also a self-contained political unit, like a country.

Civil service: The administrators and officials who run a government.

Civilization: A group of people possessing most or all of the following: a settled way of life, agriculture, a written language, an organized government, and cities.

Classical: Referring to ancient Greece and Rome.

Clergy: The priesthood.

Clerical: Relating to priests.

Coat of arms: A heraldic emblem representing a family or nation.

Commoner: Someone who is not a member of a royal or noble class.

Communion: The Christian ceremony of commemorating the last supper of Jesus Christ.

Courtly love: An idealized form of romantic love, usually of a knight or poet for a noble lady.

D

Dark Ages: A negative term sometimes used to describe the Early Middle Ages, the period from the fall of Rome to about A.D. 1000 in Western Europe.

Deity: A god.

Dialect: A regional variation on a language.

Diplomacy: The use of skillful negotiations with leaders of other nations to influence events.

Duchy: An area ruled by a duke, the highest rank of European noble below a prince.

Dynasty: A group of people, often but not always a family, who continue to hold a position of power over a period of time.

E

Economy: The whole system of production, distribution, and consumption of goods and services in a country.

Ecumenical: Across all faiths, or across all branches of the Christian Church.

Empire: A large political unit that unites many groups of people, often over a wide territory.

Epic: A long poem that recounts the adventures of a legendary hero.

Ethnic group: People who share a common racial, cultural, national, linguistic, or tribal origin.

Excommunicate: To banish someone from the church.

F

Famine: A food shortage caused by crop failures.

Fasting: Deliberately going without food, often but not always for religious reasons.

Feudalism: A form of political and economic organization in which peasants are subject to a noble who owns most or all of the land that they cultivate.

G

Geometry: A type of mathematics dealing with various shapes, their properties, and their measurements.

Guild: An association to promote, and set standards for, a particular profession or business.

H

Hajj: A pilgrimage to Mecca, which is expected of all Muslims who can afford to make it.

Heraldry: The practice of creating and studying coats of arms and other insignia.

Heresy: A belief that goes against established church teachings.

Holy Land: Palestine.

Horde: A division within the Mongol army; the term "hordes" was often used to describe the Mongol armies.

I

Icon: In the Christian church, an image of a saint.

Idol: A statue of a god that the god's followers worship.

Illumination: Decoration of a manuscript with elaborate designs.

Indo-European languages: The languages of Europe, India, Iran, and surrounding areas, which share common roots.

Indulgence: The granting of forgiveness of sins in exchange for an act of service for, or payment to, the church.

Infantry: Foot soldiers.

Infidel: An unbeliever.

Intellectual: A person whose profession or lifestyle centers around study and ideas.

Interest: In economics, a fee charged by a lender against a borrower—usually a percentage of the amount borrowed.

Investiture: The power of a feudal lord to grant lands or offices.

Islam: A religious faith that teaches submission to the one god Allah and his word as given through his prophet Muhammad in the Koran.

J

Jihad: Islamic "holy war" to defend or extend the faith.

K

Khan: A Central Asian chieftain.

Koran: The holy book of Islam.

L

Legal code: A system of laws.

Lingua franca: A common language.

M

Martyr: Someone who willingly dies for his or her faith.

Mass: A Catholic church service.

Medieval: Of or relating to the Middle Ages.

Middle Ages: Roughly the period from A.D. 500 to 1500.

Middle class: A group whose income level falls between that of the rich and the poor, or the rich and the working class; usually considered the backbone of a growing economy.

Millennium: A period of a thousand years.

Missionary: Someone who travels to other lands with the aim of converting others to his or her religion.

Monastery: A place in which monks live.

Monasticism: The tradition and practices of monks.

Monk: A man who leaves the outside world to take religious vows and live in a monastery, practicing a lifestyle of denying earthly pleasures.

Monotheism: Worship of one god.

Mosque: A Muslim temple.

Movable-type printing: An advanced printing process using pre-cast pieces of metal type.

Muezzin: A crier who calls worshipers to prayer five times a day in the Muslim world.

Mysticism: The belief that one can attain direct knowledge of God or ultimate reality through some form of meditation or special insight.

N

Nationalism: A sense of loyalty and devotion to one's nation.

Nation-state: A geographical area composed largely of a single nationality, in which a single national government clearly holds power.

New World: The Americas, or the Western Hemisphere.

Noble: A ruler within a kingdom who has an inherited title and lands but who is less powerful than the king or queen; collectively, nobles are known as the "nobility."

Nomadic: Wandering.

Novel: An extended, usually book-length, work of fiction.

Nun: The female equivalent of a monk, who lives in a nunnery, convent, or abbey.

O

Order: An organized religious community within the Catholic Church.

Ordination: Formal appointment as a priest or minister.

P

Pagan: Worshiping many gods.

Papacy: The office of the pope.

Papal: Referring to the pope.

Patriarch: A bishop in the Eastern Orthodox Church.

Patron: A supporter, particularly of arts, education, or sciences. The term is often used to refer to a ruler or wealthy person who provides economic as well as personal support.

Peasant: A farmer who works a small plot of land.

Penance: An act ordered by the church to obtain forgiveness for sin.

Persecutions: In early church history, Roman punishment of Christians for their faith.

Philosophy: An area of study concerned with subjects including values, meaning, and the nature of reality.

Pilgrimage: A journey to a site of religious significance.

Plague: A disease that spreads quickly to a large population.

Polytheism: Worship of many gods.

Pope: The bishop of Rome, and therefore the head of the Catholic Church.

Principality: An area ruled by a prince, the highest-ranking form of noble below a king.

Prophet: Someone who receives communications directly from God and passes these on to others.

Prose: Written narrative, as opposed to poetry.

Purgatory: A place of punishment after death where, according to Roman Catholic beliefs, a person who has not been damned may work out his or her salvation and earn his or her way to heaven.

R

Rabbi: A Jewish teacher or religious leader.

Racism: The belief that race is the primary factor determining peoples' abilities and that one race is superior to another.

Reason: The use of the mind to figure things out; usually contrasted with emotion, intuition, or faith.

Reformation: A religious movement in the 1500s that ultimately led to the rejection of Roman Catholicism by various groups who adopted Protestant interpretations of Christianity.

Regent: Someone who governs a country when the monarch is too young, too old, or too sick to lead.

Relic: An object associated with the saints of the New Testament or the martyrs of the early church.

Renaissance: A period of renewed interest in learning and the arts that began in Europe during the 1300s and continued to the 1600s.

Representational art: Artwork intended to show a specific subject, whether a human figure, landscape, still life, or a variation on these.

Ritual: A type of religious ceremony that is governed by very specific rules.

Rome: A term sometimes used to refer to the papacy.

S

Sack: To destroy, usually a city.

Saracen: A negative term used in medieval Europe to describe Muslims.

Scientific method: A means of drawing accurate conclusions by collecting information, studying data, and forming theories or hypotheses.

Scriptures: Holy texts.

Sect: A small group within a larger religion.

Secular: Of the world; typically used in contrast to "spiritual."

Semitic: A term describing a number of linguistic and cultural groups in the Middle East, including the modern-day Arabs and Israelis.

Serf: A peasant subject to a feudal system and possessing no land.

Siege: A sustained military attack against a city.

Simony: The practice of buying and selling church offices.

Sultan: A type of king in the Muslim world.

Sultanate: An area ruled by a Sultan.

Synagogue: A Jewish temple.

T

Technology: The application of knowledge to make the performance of physical and mental tasks easier.

Terrorism: Frightening (and usually harming) a group of people in order to achieve a specific political goal.

Theologian: Someone who analyzes religious faith.

Theology: The study of religious faith.

Trial by ordeal: A system of justice in which the accused (and sometimes the accuser as well) has to undergo various physical hardships in order to prove innocence.

Tribal: Describes a society, sometimes nomadic, in which members are organized by families and clans, not by region, and in which leadership comes from warrior-chieftains.

Tribute: Forced payments to a conqueror.

Trigonometry: The mathematical study of triangles, angles, arcs, and their properties and applications.

Trinity: The three persons of God according to Christianity—Father, Son, and Holy Spirit.

U

Usury: Loaning money for a high rate of interest; during the Middle Ages, however, it meant simply loaning money for interest.

V

Vassal: A noble or king who is subject to a more powerful noble or king.

Vatican: The seat of the pope's power in Rome.

W

West: Generally, Western Europe and North America, or the countries influenced both by ancient Greece and ancient Rome.

Working class: A group between the middle class and the poor who typically earn a living with their hands.

Joan of Arc

Born c. 1412
Died 1431

French military leader and martyr

Few people ever make history, and a person who does so in his or her teens is extremely rare. Joan of Arc, who came to prominence at the age of seventeen, never lived to see twenty. In less than three years, however, she turned the tide of a century-long conflict, and proved that a girl could lead men to victory.

Joan claimed to hear voices, which she said came from the saints, giving her wisdom from God. Whatever the source of her knowledge, she was uncannily wise beyond her years, and she might have led France to greater and greater victories if she had not been captured by her nation's enemies. Under trial as a heretic, her prophetic gift was turned against her as evidence that she was doing the Devil's work, not God's, and she was burned at the stake. The verdict of history, however, rests on the side of Joan.

The Hundred Years' War

When Joan was born in about 1412, France had been locked in a war with England for more than seventy-five

"I have come to raise the siege of Orléans and to aid you to recover your kingdom. God wills it. After I have raised the siege I will conduct you to Reims to be consecrated. Do not distress yourself over the English, for I will combat them in any place I find them."

Statement to Charles VII

Portrait: *Reproduced by permission of the Corbis Corporation.*

years. The conflict would drag on throughout her lifetime and beyond, becoming known as the Hundred Years' War (1337–1453), even though it actually lasted for 116 years.

Most of the war was fought in France, which was devastated not so much by the fighting itself—there were few actual battles during the Hundred Years' War—but by English raids on French towns. Then, in 1415, when Joan was about three years old, the English under King Henry V scored a major victory at Agincourt (AH-zhin-kohr).

After Henry died in 1422, regents who ruled England in the name of his infant son Henry VI continued the attacks. In 1428 they began a siege, or sustained assault, on the city of Orléans (ohr-lay-AWN).

Voices and visions

Joan was born in about 1412 in Domremy (doh[n]-ray-MEE), a village in the prosperous region of Champagne. Her family, despite later legends maintaining that she grew up in poverty as a shepherd girl, were in fact successful farmers.

So many tales would surround Joan's life that it was sometimes difficult to separate out the facts. For instance, artists often depicted her as possessing a physical beauty that matched her purity of spirit, but this was probably not the case. Contemporary records make no mention of her appearance (had she been a great beauty, presumably these records would have mentioned it) except to note that she was strongly and solidly built.

One thing that is known, because Joan reported it herself, was that when she was about thirteen, she began hearing voices and seeing visions. The priests at her trial would later accuse her of receiving messages from demons, and some modern scholars dismiss the voices and visions as the product of mental illness. Joan, however, claimed that she was hearing from God through the voices of long-deceased saints.

On her way to meet the king

As the siege of Orléans wore on, Joan came to believe that the voices had a special message for her. It was her destiny to save France from the English, and to do that, she needed to get the king's approval to lead an army into battle. At some point, her father tried to arrange her marriage to a local youth, but Joan had made a vow to remain a virgin, committed to Christ, and she refused.

Knowing that her father would not permit her to seek out the king, she convinced her uncle to help her get an audience with one of the local authorities. It is hard to imagine how Joan, a seventeen-year-old girl in a world where even grown women were expected to stay away from men's affairs, got anyone to take her seriously.

Finally, however, she had an opportunity to meet with Sir Robert de Baudricourt (roh-BAYR; BOH-dri-kohr), who was at first amused and then impressed by her determination. In early 1429, he arranged for her to meet with the king.

Gaining Charles's trust

In fact the king, Charles VII, had yet to be crowned. By the standards of what was required to be a king in medieval times, he was a timid figure, and later his unwillingness to make a stand would cost Joan dearly. On meeting him, Joan announced boldly that she had come to raise, or end, the siege and lead him safely to the town of Reims (RAM), the traditional place where French kings were crowned or consecrated.

Given his lack of resolve, Charles was particularly hesitant to take her claims seriously, and he forced her to undergo a series of tests concerning her faith. These tests included lengthy questioning by priests, who wanted to make sure that she was hearing from God. She passed all the tests, as she would later point out when she was brought up on charges of witchcraft.

In time Charles agreed to send her into battle, and she acquired a distinctive suit of white armor, probably made to fit a boy. As for a sword, legend holds that she told one of the king's men that he would find a specially engraved sword buried beneath the altar in a certain church—and he did. Whatever the truth of this story, it was yet another item brought up against her later as "proof" that Satan had given her special insight.

Victory after victory

To the English troops at Orléans, the sight of Joan in her white armor leading a tiny French force must have looked the way David did to Goliath in the biblical story. But just as the future king of Israel killed the giant, Joan was to lead her force to victory over a much stronger opponent. First she led the capture of the English fort at Saint Loup outside Orléans, and in a series of skirmishes, she forced the English to lift the siege. She was wounded both on the foot and above the breast, but she stayed in the battle until they had victory.

Two weeks later, Joan, claiming she had been healed by the saints, was ready to go back into action. By now she was the most popular person in France, and soldiers who had previously scorned the idea of a woman leading them into battle became zealous followers. They took the village of Patay on June 18, 1429, and their victory led a number of towns to switch their allegiance from England to France.

Joan informed Charles that he should next march on Reims, but he did not immediately heed her advice. After he relented and they began moving toward the city, they were stopped at Troyes (TRWAH), an English stronghold that they seemingly could not conquer. With supplies running out, the men were starting to grow hungry, but Joan urged them not to give up the siege, telling the troops that they would have victory in just two more days. Once again she was proven right, and on July 17, 1429, Charles was crowned in Reims with Joan standing nearby.

Trouble on the horizon

Charles and the leaders of the French army never fully accepted Joan into their confidence and often excluded her from strategy meetings. In many cases they would seek her advice after having met amongst themselves, only to discover that they should have asked her in the first place.

Joan's extremely unorthodox ways were bound to make her enemies, and not just on the English side. Many of the French remained uncomfortable with the idea of a female leader, and civilians as well as soldiers remarked scornfully about her habit of always wearing men's clothes. Nonethe-

less, she had far more admirers than opponents among the French, and everywhere she went, crowds tried to touch her in the hopes that she could heal sicknesses—a gift she never claimed.

Then in September 1429, she failed to take Paris, and was wounded again, this time in the leg. Two months later, she failed to take another town. Meanwhile, she was growing restless with Charles's indecisiveness; therefore she set out to assist the fortress at Compiegne (kawn-pee-AN) in the northeast, which was under attack. It was to be her last military campaign.

Capture and trial

During a battle in May 1430, Joan was captured by John of Luxembourg, who was loyal to the Duchy of Burgundy. Burgundy, a large state to the north of France, was in

Joan of Arc (on horseback) led French troops to many victories in battle against their English enemies.

William Wallace

Like Joan, William Wallace (c. 1270–1305), subject of the 1995 Academy Award–winning film *Braveheart,* led a heroic struggle against the English on behalf of his people. As with Joan, his fight was to end in his own trial and execution—but he, too, would remain a powerful symbol.

A minor Scottish nobleman from the western part of the country, William grew up in a time when his land faced severe oppression from the English. In his early twenties, he became the leader of a rag-tag guerrilla army that set out to oppose them.

With the support of the lower classes and the lesser nobility—but not the greater nobles, who favored coexistence with their English masters—William led what was called the Rising of 1297. They scored a major victory against the armies of King Edward I at Stirling Bridge on September 11, but were badly defeated at Falkirk on July 22 of the following year.

In the wake of Falkirk, William fled the country, going to France and Italy in hopes of gaining support for a new campaign against Edward. He never obtained it, and on August 5, 1305, after he had returned to Scotland, one of his former lieutenants turned him over to the English.

William Wallace. *Reproduced by permission of Archive Photos, Inc.*

William was tried for war and treason, and as with Joan, the results of the trial were a foregone conclusion. Dragged by horses to the gallows, he was hanged and then disemboweled (his intestines were removed). Edward ordered William's severed head to be placed on display on London Bridge, and sent his body in pieces to be displayed at four castles around Scotland. His move backfired, however: the murder of William became a rallying cry for the Scots, who soon raised a much more formidable effort against England.

turn allied with the English, to whom they gave her after receiving a handsome payment. The English were thrilled, and immediately handed her over to Peter Cauchon (koh-SHAWn), bishop of Beauvais (boh-VAY), for trial. Neither

Charles nor any of the other French leaders made any significant effort to rescue her.

The legal proceedings that followed represented a ghastly miscarriage of justice, even by medieval standards. Because she was charged with heresy, or defying church teachings, she should have been confined in a jail controlled by the church, where she would have had female guards. Instead, she was thrown into a dungeon controlled by the civil authorities in the town of Rouen (rü-AN), and there she was guarded by five of the most brutish soldiers the English could muster.

Her trial wore on for months and months, and Cauchon's tactics failed to wrangle a confession from Joan. He and the other interrogators could never successfully tie her to witchcraft, and eventually the charges were whittled down to a claim that she was not cooperating with the trial. Scrambling to find a case, Cauchon emphasized her wearing of men's clothing as evidence of her disloyalty to the church. Finally on May 24, 1431, he managed to bully the exhausted Joan into signing a statement that she was guilty of a wide range of crimes. She even agreed to wear women's clothing.

The martyrdom of Joan

Cauchon had led Joan to believe that after signing the statement, she would be moved to a church prison. Instead, he had her thrown back into the dungeon. Realizing that she would never get out alive, she made a final act of protest by putting on men's clothing again. Now Cauchon had her where he wanted her: not only was she a heretic, but she had gone back to her heresy after recanting, or disavowing, it.

On May 30, Joan's death sentence was read aloud in the town square of Rouen. Her captors were so eager to see her killed that, in another breach of law—the church had no power to pass a death sentence in France—they immediately hauled her off to her execution. She was tied to a pole, and branches were heaped around her; then the fire was lit, and Joan was burned at the stake.

The English and their French allies—most of those involved in the trial were her countrymen—were so afraid of Joan and her alleged witchcraft that they arranged to have her ashes thrown in the River Seine nearby. And indeed Joan did exert a force after her death: her efforts contributed significantly to France's final victory in 1453.

By that time there was a massive movement to reverse the sentence against Joan. In 1456, a commission directed by Pope Calixtus III declared that the verdict against her had been wrongfully obtained. Joan soon became one of the most widely loved and admired figures in Europe, and in 1920, she was declared a saint.

For More Information

Books

Bull, Angela. *A Saint in Armor: The Story of Joan of Arc.* New York: Dorling Kindersley Publishers, 2000.

Bunson, Margaret and Matthew. *St. Joan of Arc.* Huntington, IN: Our Sunday Visitor, 1992.

Hodges, Margaret. *Joan of Arc: The Lily Maid.* Illustrated by Robert Rayevsky. New York: Holiday House, 1999.

Madison, Lucy Foster. *Joan of Arc.* Retold by Christine Messina, illustrations by Frank Schoonover. New York: Children's Classics, 1995.

Nardo, Don. *The Trial of Joan of Arc.* San Diego, CA: Lucent Books, 1998.

Web Sites

"Joan of Arc" (1452–1519). [Online] Available http://www.phs.princeton.k12.oh.us/Public/Lessons/enl/sudz2.html (last accessed July 26, 2000).

ScotWeb's Scottish History Online Magazine. [Online] Available http://www.clan.com/history/mainframe.html (last accessed July 26, 2000).

"The Trial of Scotsman William Wallace, 1306." *World Wide Legal Information Association.* [Online] Available http://www.wwlia.org/uk-wall.htm (last accessed July 26, 2000).

William Wallace: The Truth. [Online] Available http://www.highlander-web.co.uk/wallace/index2.html (last accessed July 26, 2000).

Justinian

Born 483
Died 565

Byzantine emperor

The Byzantine Empire, which grew out of the Eastern Roman Empire in Greece, carried Roman culture into the Middle Ages. It was a splendid and sometimes powerful realm, a stronghold of civilization in a dark time, and Justinian was perhaps its greatest ruler.

Justinian reconquered the Western Roman Empire, which had fallen to invading tribes in 476, and briefly reunited former Roman lands under his leadership. More lasting was his legal code, or system of laws, which provided the foundation for much of the law that exists today. Justinian built dozens of churches, most notably the Hagia Sophia in Constantinople, and under his reign, Byzantine arts—including mosaics, colored bits of glass or tile arranged to form a picture—reached a high point.

In his uncle's care

The Byzantine (BIZ-un-teen) Empire, sometimes known as Byzantium (bi-ZAN-tee-um), controlled much of southeastern Europe, western Asia, and northern Africa from

"If you wish to save yourself, Sire, it can easily be done.... For my own part, I hold to the old saying that the imperial purple makes the best burial sheet!"

Theodora, urging Justinian to take action during the Nika Revolt of 532

its capital at Constantinople (kahn-stan-ti-NOH-pul), which today is the city of Istanbul in Turkey. Justinian, however, grew up far from the centers of power, in a village called Tauresium. His family had been humble farmers just a generation before, but his uncle Justin (c. 450–527) had changed their fortunes when he went to Constantinople and became a member of the imperial bodyguard charged with protecting the life of Emperor Leo I.

Eventually Justin became commander of the imperial guards and a military leader of distinction. Having no children of his own, Justin brought his nephews—including Justinian—to Constantinople, where he helped them gain an education and embark on careers. Justinian enjoyed the benefits of a superb education, something Justin, who never learned to read and write, did not have. As was the Roman custom (the Byzantines referred to themselves as "Romans"), Justinian proved his ability by service in the military.

Co-ruler and sole ruler

In 518, the reigning emperor died, and Justin was chosen as his successor. Now the uncle called on his nephews, who had the education he lacked, to assist him in leading the empire, and none of these men distinguished himself more than Justinian. The latter became one of Justin's key advisors, and early in Justin's reign uncovered a plot against his uncle by one of the emperor's rivals.

Although Justinian was in his late thirties by now, Justin formally adopted him at some point during the 520s as a means of preparing to pass on leadership to him. In 525, the emperor designated his nephew as his preferred successor, though under the Roman system, succession was far from automatic: the emperor's chosen successor had to prove himself. Evidently Justinian did, because Justin promoted him to co-emperor on April 4, 527, and when the uncle died on August 1, Justinian became sole ruler.

Marriage to Theodora

Justinian had passed the age of forty before marrying, and when he did marry, it required the changing of an ancient Roman law. The reason was that the woman with whom he chose to share his life, Theodora (see box), was an actress—and in the Byzantine world, actresses had positions in society similar to that of prostitutes (and in fact, many actresses *were* prostitutes). Men of Justinian's class were forbidden from marrying women such as Theodora. Therefore Justinian, who fell deeply and passionately in love with the young woman (she was half his age) after meeting her in 522, had prevailed on Justin to strike down the old Roman law. Thus Justinian and Theodora were able to marry in 525.

Justinian and Theodora would gain enemies, among them the historian Procopius (pruh-KOH-pee-us), whose book *Secret History* portrays them as scheming villains. Although many aspects of Procopius's book are unfair, it is true that they reigned as co-rulers, with the wife sometimes exercising more influence than the husband. Despite Theodora's checkered past, to which Procopius devoted several gossipy, scandalous chapters, not even he could claim that she was ever unfaithful to Justinian after their marriage. It appears that they enjoyed a very happy married life, and that the empress proved a great asset to her husband.

The turning point

Theodora demonstrated her importance to the emperor during the Nika Revolt of 532, when Constantinople was nearly destroyed by rioters. Byzantine society was dominated by two rival groups called the Greens and the Blues, distinguished by the colors of horse-racing teams that competed at the Hippodrome, or stadium. Justinian and Theodora favored the Blues, and when he made an appearance in their company at the Hippodrome on January 13, 532, this sparked a riot. Suddenly the Greens attacked the Blues, chanting a favorite cheer from the races: "*Nika!*" (Conquer!). Constantinople was plunged into five days of bloodshed, fires, and looting, which very nearly destroyed the city and toppled Justinian's government. By January 18, leaders of the Blues and Greens, realizing that Justinian's high taxes were the source of all their troubles, had joined forces against Justinian, and were ready to storm the palace.

Theodora sat by in silence while Justinian's advisors suggested that he try to escape the city. Then she stood and

Detail of a mosaic of empress Theodora from the Church of San Vitale at Ravenna, Italy. Byzantine arts—particularly mosaics—flourished under Justinian's rule. *Reproduced by permission of the Library of Congress.*

addressed the imperial council with one of the most remarkable speeches in history. "It is impossible for a man, once born, not to die," she said, and went on to remind her husband that with the great wealth of the imperial court, they could easily escape. But, she said, she agreed with a saying of the ancient orator Isocrates (eye-SAHK-ruh-teez; 436–338 B.C.) "that the imperial purple makes the best burial sheet"—in other words, that it is better to die a king than to live as a coward. Justinian was moved to action by Theodora's speech, and he sent an army led by his great general Belisarius (c. 505–565) to crush the rioters. The soldiers ruthlessly slaughtered more than thirty thousand people in the Hippodrome.

The Nika Revolt was a critical turning point in Justinian's reign because his response to it (thanks to his wife and his general) helped him gain a firm grip on power. Also in 532, Byzantium signed a peace agreement with an age-old enemy to the east, Persia (modern-day Iran). This gave Justinian the freedom to turn westward and pursue his greatest ambition: the reunification of the Roman Empire.

Wars of conquest

Led by Belisarius, the Byzantine armies in 534 won back North Africa from the Vandals, a tribe who had taken the region from Rome more than a century before. Thus he prepared the way for Justinian's primary aim, the reconquest of Italy from another tribe, the Ostrogoths. In 535, Belisarius conquered the island of Sicily, just off the Italian coast, and by 536, controlled the city of Rome itself.

After four bitter years of war, the Ostrogoths tried to crown Belisarius himself as "Emperor of the Western Empire," but Belisarius double-crossed them, and claimed all of Italy for Justinian in 540. The Ostrogoths responded by sending a message to Khosrow (kawz-ROW; ruled 531–79), the king of Persia, initiating a two-pronged offensive against the Byzantines. The Persians took several key cities, and this forced Justinian to send Belisarius eastward to deal with the Persian threat.

Without Belisarius in Italy, Rome and other cities fell back into the hands of the Ostrogoths. In 550, however, Justinian sent a new general, Narses (NAR-seez; c. 480–574), to conquer Italy. Over the course of the next thirteen years, he subdued the Ostrogoths and their allies, but in so doing he practically destroyed Italy; nevertheless, the Byzantines, who had also won back southern Spain, now controlled a large part of the former Roman Empire.

Detail of a famous mosaic of Justinian from the Church of San Vitale in Italy.
Reproduced by permission of the Granger Collection Ltd.

Though Justinian spent most of his energy waging his wars of conquest, those wars were far from clear-cut successes. Not only did he cause great destruction to Italy itself, but he became intensely involved in the religious politics there, removing one pope in favor of another, and ordering the deaths of people who opposed his views on religion. Furthermore, the effort was hardly worth it: except for parts of Italy, the Byzantines lost most of the reconquered lands within a few years of Justinian's death.

Laws and buildings

Justinian's importance as a leader lies not in his record as a conqueror, but in his contributions to civilization. Early in his reign, he had begun the project of reforming Byzantine law, which had become hopelessly complicated over the centuries. Looking back to ancient Roman models, Justinian's appointed legal authority, Tribonian, greatly sim-

Theodora

The empress Theodora (c. 500–548) came from far more humble beginnings than her husband, Justinian. Born somewhere in the east, perhaps Syria, she grew up in Constantinople. Her family was extremely poor and had to rely on the kindness of others to survive.

In the Byzantine rivalry between two opposing groups, the Greens and the Blues, Theodora became a lifelong supporter of the Blues, but not for any political reasons. Her father Athanasius had worked in the Hippodrome as a bear-keeper for the Greens, but he died when Theodora and her two sisters were very young. Her mother quickly remarried, and Theodora's stepfather tried to take over Athanasius's old job. The man in charge of assigning the positions, however, had accepted a bribe to give it to someone else, and no amount of pleading on the mother's part could sway the Greens. The Blues, however, saw this as an opportunity to shame the Greens, and gave the stepfather a job.

Times were extremely hard for Theodora and her family, but she was a talented and extraordinarily beautiful young woman. She started out acting in mime shows at the Hippodrome, but soon she was performing in the nude, and eventually she followed her older sister in becoming a prostitute. Unlike modern America, where actors and actresses are respected members of society, in Byzantium actresses were lowly members of society, partly because many of them were prostitutes.

At the age of sixteen, Theodora became the lover of a powerful man named Hecebolus (hek-EB-uh-lus). Appointed governor of a province in North Africa, Hecebolus took her with him, but after four years he left her, penniless and far from home. She spent the next year working her way back home, once again plying her trade as a prostitute.

But something remarkable happened in the Egyptian city of Alexandria, where she came in contact with a form of Christianity called the Monophysite (muh-NAH-fu-syt) faith. Whereas mainstream Christianity taught that Jesus Christ was both God and man, the Monophysites be-

plified the system, creating a code that established the basis for much of modern law.

Another area of great achievement during Justinian's reign was in the arts. Among the few lasting reminders of the Byzantine presence in Italy, for instance, is the Church of San Vitale in Italy, a gorgeous piece of architecture that later inspired **Charlemagne** (see entry) in the building of his own

lieved that he was *only* God. Theodora did not care about religious distinctions, however: what drew her to the Monophysites was that, unlike many mainstream Christians at the time, their ministers preached directly to women. She became a Christian, renounced her former lifestyle, and in 522 returned to Constantinople. There she settled in a house near the palace, and made a living spinning wool.

Also in 522, she met Justinian, a man old enough to be her father. He fell madly in love with her and arranged for his uncle, the emperor Justin, to change the laws preventing men of the upper classes from marrying actresses and prostitutes. They were married in 525, and appear to have had an extremely happy married life. When Justinian became co-emperor with Justin on April 4, 527, Theodora accompanied her husband to the Hippodrome, where they were greeted by cheering crowds. It must have been a moving experience for her, now an empress, to visit that place where, as a girl, she had been a lowly performer.

Throughout the two decades that followed, Theodora exercised considerable influence over Justinian, and sometimes seemed to hold greater power than he. She rightly saw that the empire's real interests lay in the east, rather than in Italy, which Justinian reconquered at great cost. She also pushed for laws that improved the status of women, for instance by prohibiting forced prostitution. Furthermore, she helped protect the Monophysites from persecution by mainstream Christians; but perhaps the greatest example of Theodora's leadership was her role during the Nika Revolt.

Theodora's advice about how to handle the rioters moved Justinian to order his general Belisarius to put down the revolt. In the bloody aftermath, Justinian emerged as absolute ruler over Byzantium. He could never have enjoyed such great power without his wife, a woman as renowned for her wisdom as for her beauty. When she died of cancer on June 28, 548, Justinian was heartbroken.

chapel at Aachen. The interior of San Vitale contains mosaics depicting Justinian and Theodora, and these portraits are perhaps the two most famous artworks from Byzantium's 1,100-year history.

Certainly the most well-known Byzantine structure is the Hagia (HAH-juh) Sophia, one of more than thirty churches in Constantinople built under Justinian's orders following

An aerial view of the Hagia Sophia, completed in 537 under Justinian's orders, in what is now Istanbul, Turkey. *Photograph by Yann Arthus-Bertrand. Reproduced by permission of the Corbis Corporation.*

the Nika Revolt. Completed in 537, the church is dominated by a dome that, despite its enormous size—184 feet high and 102 feet wide—seemed to one observer in Justinian's time as though it were "suspended by a gold chain from heaven."

Justinian's last years

Between his wars and his building projects, Justinian ran up enormous expenses, which he attempted to pay for through high taxes on his people. Taxes under Justinian were so high that many people lost everything—another cause for bitterness on the part of Procopius and others.

In 548, Justinian lost his beloved Theodora to cancer, and his last years were lonely ones. In 562, the uncovering of an assassination plot against him made him aware of the need to choose a successor; but like Justin, he had no children of his own. Therefore he promoted his second cousin and nephew, both named Justin, into positions from which either could succeed him as emperor. After he died on November 14, 565, at the age of eighty-three—extraordinarily old for the time—his nephew took the throne.

For More Information

Books

Chrisp, Peter. *The World of the Roman Emperor.* New York: P. Bedrick Books, 1999.

Nardo, Don. *Rulers of Ancient Rome.* San Diego, CA: Lucent Books, 1999.

Web Sites

"The Empress Theodora." [Online] Available http://www.campus.north-park.edu/history/Webchron/EastEurope/Theodora.html (last accessed July 26, 2000).

Imperium. [Online] Available http://www.ghgcorp.com/shetler/oldimp/ (last accessed July 26, 2000).

"Theodora." [Online] Available http://www.komets.k12.mn.us/faculty/Simmon's%20Students/Rhoten's%20Internet%20Page/Theodora.html (last accessed July 26, 2000).

"Theodora (500–548)." [Online] Available http://members.home.com/cheree/theo.html (last accessed July 26, 2000).

Kublai Khan

Born 1215
Died 1294

Mongol ruler of China

Though he belonged to the Mongol nation, conquerors of half the known world, Kublai Khan is remembered more for his peacetime activities than for his record as a warrior. Grandson of the fierce **Genghis Khan** (see entry), Kublai himself subdued China and established that nation's first foreign-dominated dynasty, the Yüan (yee-WAHN). But he was also an enthusiastic supporter of the arts and sciences, and through his contact with **Marco Polo** (see entry), he became widely known in the Western world.

Genghis and Kublai

Khan is a term for a chieftain in Central Asia, home of the Mongol people. The Mongols were a nomadic, or wandering, nation that had little effect on world events until the time of Genghis Khan (JING-us; c. 1162–1227), Kublai's grandfather. Genghis led them on a series of conquests that would make the Mongols rulers over the largest empire in history.

In the year of Kublai's birth, Genghis destroyed the city known today as Beijing (bay-ZHEENG). The Mongols,

"The greatest Lord that is now in the world or ever has been."

Marco Polo

Portrait: *Reproduced by permission of the New York Public Library Picture Collection.*

who began rebuilding it as their own headquarters in China, named it Khanbalik (kahn-bah-LEEK), and it was from there that Kublai would one day rule. Twelve years later, Genghis died, having divided his lands among his three sons. Kublai himself became ruler over a large area in northern China when he was sixteen years old.

Descendants of Genghis

Over the years that followed, leadership of the Mongols would pass from one to another of Genghis's descendants, and during this time the empire became more and more divided. Genghis's son Ogodai ruled from 1229 to 1241, during which time he expanded the Mongol conquests into Eastern Europe. Five years would pass between his death and the election of a new khan, Kuyuk, in 1246. Kuyuk lived only two more years, and it took the Mongols three additional years to choose another khan, his cousin (and Kublai's older brother) Mangu.

Mangu ruled from 1251 to 1259, during which time his cousin Hulagu invaded Persia and Mesopotamia (modern-day Iran and Iraq). After Mangu died, Hulagu declared himself "Il-khan," and from then on, southwestern Asia would be a separate khanate (KAHN-et) under the rule of Hulagu and his descendants. By that time, Kublai was forty-four years old. Little is known about his life up to this point, but he was about to emerge onto center-stage.

Kublai becomes Great Khan

In the years after Genghis's death, four separate khanates emerged: the Il-Khanate in Southwest Asia; the Chagatai (chah-guh-TY) khanate in Central Asia; the Golden Horde in Russia; and the lands of the Great Khan. The latter was the most important part of the Mongol empire, comprising the Mongolian homeland and the Mongols' most prized possession, China. Whoever ruled this area was considered the true ruler of all the Mongols.

In 1260, Kublai was busy in southern China, fighting against the armies of the Sung dynasty. The latter, which had ruled the land since 960, still controlled the southern part of China, and the Mongols considered it essential to destroy this last holdout of Chinese resistance. It was while Kublai was leading armies against the Sung that he was proclaimed Great Khan, on May 5, 1260.

A month later, Kublai's younger brother Arigböge (ur-ug-BOH-guh) declared himself Great Khan with the support of many Mongol leaders. The latter believed that Kublai had been too influenced by Chinese ways, and had become too soft to call himself a Mongol. Yet Kublai proved his strength as leader when he managed to surround Arigböge's forces and prevent supplies from reaching them. By 1264, Arigböge had surrendered.

Conquering China

Now as the undisputed Great Khan, Kublai turned his attention to eliminating the Sung Chinese. Since southern China, with its hills and marshes, was not suited to the Mongols' usual horsebound fighting force, Kublai had to build up a navy, something the Mongols had never possessed. They had their first significant victory over the Sung in 1265, and from 1268 to 1273, they concentrated on subduing two cities on the Han River that had so far resisted them. Victory over those strongholds gave them access to the river, and in 1275 they won a massive naval battle.

The emperor of China was a four-year-old boy, and his grandmother ruled in his place as a regent. She tried to arrange a compromise with Kublai Khan, but the Great Khan had no interest in compromising. By 1279, the Sung had surrendered, and Kublai's Yüan dynasty controlled all of China.

China under the rule of the Great Khan

Kublai proved a wise and capable leader: rather than crush the Chinese, he allowed their cities to remain standing, and sought their help in running the country. He put in place a number of agencies to ensure that all the people received equal treatment, and that corruption did not flourish within the government. The Mongols in general, and Kublai in particular, tended to be open-minded in matters of culture and religion, especially because they did not have a well-developed civilization that they intended to impose on others by force. Thus they allowed a number of religions to flourish, including Nestorian Christianity (see box).

It should be stressed, however, that the Mongols *were* conquerors, and some of the fiercest warriors in history. China's population dropped dramatically during the time of the Mongols' invasion and subsequent rule, and though this can partly be attributed to natural disasters, some of the blame has to rest with the Mongols themselves.

Given the Mongol record of conquest and bloodshed, then, Kublai's embracing of civilization is all the more remarkable. Not only did he promote the arts and sciences, but he created a highly advanced legal code, or set of laws, and attempted unsuccessfully to impose an alphabet that would make translation between Chinese and other languages easier.

Marco Polo

Kublai also encouraged trade with other lands, and in particular opened up paths between Europe and East Asia. Under his reign, a network of postal stations that doubled as travelers' inns dotted the route between East and West. As a result of Kublai's opening of trade routes, Marco Polo arrived along with his uncle and father.

The Italian journeyer would later write a record of his travels, in which he immortalized Kublai Khan as the greatest ruler on Earth. Marco Polo praised the Great Khan's brilliance as a leader, and celebrated the wealth of his kingdom. Yet during Polo's stay in China, which lasted from 1275 to 1292, Kublai Khan's reign reached its peak and then began a steady decline.

Foreign troubles

Perhaps because he was eager to prove himself as a conqueror, and thus to establish his reputation as a "true" Mongol, Kublai had been attempting to subdue Japan since 1266. In the meantime, he had won control of Korea in 1273. A year later, a force composed of some 29,000 Mongol, Chi-

Rabban Bar Sauma

Many people know about visits to China by medieval European travelers, the most famous of whom was Marco Polo; much less well known were travelers from the East who went to Europe. Among these, perhaps the most notable example was Rabban Bar Sauma (ruh-BAHN BAR sah-OO-muh; c. 1220–1294).

Bar Sauma came from the Uighur (WEE-gur), a Turkic nation under the rule of the Mongols. He was born in Khanbalik, and embraced Nestorianism, a branch of Christianity that had split from the mainstream Christian church in A.D. 431. Since that time, Nestorianism had flourished mainly in the East.

At the age of twenty, Bar Sauma became a Nestorian monk and began to preach the Christian message, attracting many followers. Among these was a young man named Mark. The latter accompanied Bar Sauma when, at about the age of fifty-five, he made a pilgrimage or religious journey to Jerusalem.

They went with the blessing of Kublai Khan, and met with the catholicos, the leader of the Nestorian church, in what is now Iran. He in turn sent them as ambassadors to the Il-Khan, a relative of Kublai Khan who ruled Persia. Later Mark became a bishop, and when the catholicos died, he took his place.

A new leader of the Il-Khanate in 1284 wanted European help against the Muslim Arabs of the Middle East, and he sent Bar Sauma westward to seek their aid. Bar Sauma departed from what is now Iraq in 1287, and as he later wrote in the record of his travels, he visited the Byzantine Empire before arriving in Italy. There he hoped to meet with the pope, leader of the Catholic Church, but the old pope was dead and he had to wait for the election of a new one.

While he waited, Bar Sauma traveled throughout Western Europe, visiting parts of Italy and France. Back in Rome in 1288, he met the new pope, Nicholas IV, who expressed an interest in joining the Il-Khan in a war against the Muslims. This never happened, but Bar Sauma (who died in 1294 in Baghdad, now a city in Iraq) helped open the way for more travelers between East and West.

nese, and Korean soldiers crossed the Korean Strait to Japan, but a storm destroyed many of their boats, and the surviving troops headed back to China.

At the same time, Kublai faced a threat on his western border from his cousin Khaidu (KY-dü), ruler of the Chagatai

English poet Samuel Taylor Coleridge (1772–1834) immortalized Kublai Khan in his poem of the same name written in 1816. *Drawing by J. Kayser.*

khanate. Not only did Khaidu's rivalry force Kublai to devote troops to defending the western frontier of his empire, it also ended any illusions Kublai may have had concerning a great Mongol alliance. Clearly the realms won by his grandfather would never again be a single entity with a single ruler, and no doubt this fact made Kublai all the more determined to conquer Japan for himself.

After the Japanese murdered two of his ambassadors in 1279, Kublai sent some 150,000 troops to Japan. In August 1281, a typhoon—that is, a great storm on the Pacific Ocean—struck the Mongol ships and killed more than half of their fighting force. The Japanese praised the typhoon as a gift from the gods, and the loss was a devastating blow to the Mongols: clearly it was possible for them to lose, and indeed they would get considerably more experience at losing in coming years.

The 1280s saw a failed campaign in Annam and Champa, which constituted what is now Vietnam; and in 1290, Tibet revolted against Mongol rule. The Mongols put down the rebellion, but only at a great cost, and in 1293 they failed to conquer the island of Java in modern-day Indonesia.

The Great Khan's last days

By the time Marco Polo left China, Kublai Khan was nearing the end of his life. His last days were not happy ones, and in addition to military problems, he faced personal devastation when both his favorite wife and his son were killed. He suffered from gout, a disease that makes the body's joints stiff and inflamed, and heavy drinking only added to his health problems. A combination of alcoholism and depression, which probably caused him to overeat, made the Great

Khan extremely overweight. He died on February 18, 1294, at the age of eighty.

The Chinese had never accustomed themselves to foreign rule, and without Kublai's strong influence, the Yüan dynasty soon lost power. In 1368 it was overthrown, and eventually the Mongols themselves faded into the shadows of history. By the twentieth century, Mongolia was one of the most sparsely populated countries on Earth, and hardly seemed like a nation that had once ruled the world.

Yet thanks to Marco Polo and others, the memory of Kublai would live on. More than five hundred years after the Great Khan's death, the English poet Samuel Taylor Coleridge immortalized him in the poem "Kubla Khan" (1816), which began with a reference to "Xanadu" (ZAN-uh-doo). The latter was Shang-tu, a great city built by Kublai, a city whose remains have long since all but disappeared.

For More Information

Books

Dramer, Kim. *Kublai Khan*. New York: Chelsea House, 1990.

Ganeri, Anita. *Marco Polo*. Illustrated by Ross Watton. New York: Dillon Press, 1999.

Martell, Hazel. *Imperial China, 221 b.c. to a.d. 1294*. Austin, TX: Raintree Steck-Vaughn Publishers, 1999.

Silverberg, Robert. *Kublai Khan, Lord of Xanadu*. Indianapolis, IN: Bobbs-Merrill, 1966.

Web Sites

"Ancient China: The Mongolian Empire: The Yuan Dynasty, 1279–1368." [Online] Available http://www.wsu.edu:8080/~dee/CHEMPIRE/YUAN.HTM (last accessed July 26, 2000).

"Marko Polo—Million." [Online] Available http://www.korcula.net/mpolo/mpolo5.htm (last accessed July 26, 2000).

"Old World Contacts/Armies/Kublai Khan." *University of Calgary*. [Online] Available http://www.ucalgary.ca/HIST/tutor/oldwrld/armies/kublai.html (last accessed July 26, 2000).

Leif Eriksson

Born c. 970
Died c. 1020

Viking explorer

A lmost five hundred years before Christopher Columbus's ships landed in the New World, Leif Eriksson and his crew of Vikings became the first Europeans to reach North America. As was the case with Columbus later, they had no idea where they were—except that they knew they had found a land rich in natural resources. But whereas Columbus and others who followed possessed firearms, giving them military superiority over the Native Americans, the Vikings had no such advantage. Therefore they did not conquer the lands they discovered; but there is virtually no doubt that they set foot on them.

"There was dew on the grass, and the first thing they did was to get some of it on their hands and put it to their lips, and to them it seemed the sweetest thing they had ever tasted."

Description of Markland, from Erik the Red's Saga

Iceland

One cannot discuss the career of Leif Eriksson (LAYF) without referring to that of his father, Erik the Red. Erik was a Viking, born in Norway in about 950. By that time, groups of Vikings—sometimes called Norsemen or Northmen—had long since fanned out from their homeland in Scandinavia. They committed murder and mayhem in Ireland, which they attacked in about 800, and various other Vikings spread to

Russia, where they became known as Varangians, as well as to France and Sicily, where they were called Normans.

In 860, the Vikings discovered an island far to the northwest of Ireland. Because the place was lush and fertile and they feared overpopulation—the reason they had left Scandinavia in the first place—the explorers gave it the forbidding-sounding name of Iceland. It was to Iceland that Erik's family went in his childhood, after his father was forced to leave Norway.

Greenland

Beyond Iceland was another island about 175 miles away, close enough that it could be seen on clear days. This uninviting land had been named Greenland in the hopes that settlers might bypass Iceland for Greenland's supposedly fertile lands. When he grew up, Erik, like his father, managed to run into trouble, and decided to take his family to Greenland in 981.

He had been drawn partly by tales of wealthy Irish settlers there, but when he reached the island he found that he and those with him were the only people. They continued to explore, sailing as far west as Baffin Island, now part of Canada. At that time both Baffin Island and Greenland supported much more life than they do now, and the Vikings lived well.

They settled in Greenland, where in 986 Erik founded a permanent settlement. Around this time, a Viking named Bjarni Herjolfsson (BYAR-nee HUR-julf-sun) was sailing from Iceland to Greenland when his ship was blown off course. Historians now believe that he was the first European to catch sight of North America, but he did not land. That feat would be accomplished a few years later by Erik's son.

North America

Leif was one of four children, all of whom would one day travel to North America. Unlike his father, who clung to the Vikings' old pagan traditions, Leif accepted Christianity and is credited with bringing the religion to Greenland. In

1001, when he was about thirty years old, he sailed westward with a crew of thirty-five.

It is believed that Leif's crew landed first on the southern part of Baffin Island, then sailed to the coast of Labrador on the Canadian mainland. There they landed on what may have been Belle Isle, an island between Labrador and Newfoundland that they dubbed Markland, or "forest land." From there they went on to a place they called Vinland, or "land of the vine" (grapes)—probably a spot on Newfoundland's northeastern tip. There they established a settlement they called Leifrsbudir (LAYFRS-boo-deer), "Leif's booths."

Leif Eriksson stands at the head of a boat off the coast of Vinland, which was probably located at the northeastern tip of what is now Newfoundland, Canada. *Reproduced by permission of the Corbis Corporation.*

Later journeys of Leif's siblings

Leif's party returned to Greenland in 1002, but his brother Thorvald made a journey to Vinland that lasted from 1003 to 1005. They fought with Native Americans,

Other Medieval Explorers and Geographers

The Middle Ages are not commonly considered a time of great exploration, yet the era produced a number of great journeyers, among them **Marco Polo**, Ibn Battuta, Cheng Ho, and Rabban Bar Sauma (see Marco Polo entry and boxes in Marco Polo, Henry the Navigator, and Kublai Khan entries, respectively). In addition to these were a host of other explorers and geographers.

Hsüan-tsang (shooy-AHND ZAHNG; 602–664) was not the first Chinese journeyer to visit India, but his travels were notable due to their enormous cultural significance. A Buddhist monk, Hsüan-tsang wanted to study the religion in the land where it was born, so in 629 he set off alone. Travel into China's western regions was forbidden under the T'ang dynasty, so he slipped across the border, making a perilous journey across what is now southern Russia, Afghanistan, and Pakistan. He was the first Chinese traveler to visit all the major regions of India, where he had many adventures. He studied for a time in a Buddhist school, and he visited the courts of Harsha (see box in Mansa Musa entry) and other kings. He brought back Buddhist scriptures that helped lead to the expansion of the religion in China, and he remains a celebrated figure whose deeds are recorded in Chinese operas, paintings, films, and even comic books.

Al-Idrisi (1100–c. 1165) was a journeyer, but his greatest significance to medieval exploration lies in his work as a geographer. Born in Morocco, he visited Asia Minor (modern-day Turkey), North Africa, Spain, France, and perhaps even England before reaching Sicily, where he found his life's work. In 1144 Roger II, the island's Norman king, commissioned al-Idrisi to oversee the creation of a massive work of geography that came to be known as the *Book of Roger.* The latter represented the cutting edge of geographical knowledge in its time.

Like al-Idrisi, Yaqut (yah-KÜT; 1179–1229) is remembered as much for his scholarship as for his journeys. Born a slave in Syria, he was freed when he was in his

who they called "skraelings," and Thorvald was killed by an arrow. In 1006, Thorvald's crew sailed home, but another brother, Thorstein, returned to the area to recover Thorvald's body. He ran into storms and died upon his return to Greenland.

In 1010, Leif's brother-in-law, Thorfinn, who had married Thorstein's widow, Gudrid, founded a settlement on Vinland. Gudrid and the other females on this voyage were the first European women in North America, and her son

Hsüan-tsang. *Reproduced by permission of the Granger Collection Ltd.*

of the last Islamic scholars to have access to libraries in Central Asia that were destroyed by the Mongol invasions soon afterward.

Despite the losses caused by the Mongols, their conquests also opened the way for the eastward journeys of Europeans such as Marco Polo and "Sir John Mandeville." Actually, Sir John probably never lived—but that did not stop *The Voyage and Travels of Sir John Mandeville, Knight* from becoming a medieval best-seller. Published in about 1360, the book contained a record of journeys through Asia, including a detailed report on the lands of Prester John, a Christian king to the East who had been rumored to exist for centuries. Dreams of finding Prester John's kingdom, as well as other fantastic lands described by Sir John Mandeville, helped drive Europeans in their quest for exploration that began in the mid-1400s. Thus it can be said that the fictitious Sir John, whose book may have been written by a doctor in Liège (lee-EZH, now part of Belgium), also contributed to geographical knowledge in a roundabout way.

twenties and began wide-ranging journeys that took him all the way from the Arabian Peninsula to Central Asia. His book *Kitab mu'jam al-buldan* is among the first organized, scholarly works of geography to combine history, culture, and science in a consistent structure. Yaqut's writing is particularly significant due to the fact that he was one

Snorri, born in the summer of 1011, was the first European child born on the continent. The Norsemen traded furs with the skraelings, but later they fell into conflict, and warfare drove them back to Greenland.

Leif's half-sister, Freydis (illegitimate daughter of Erik), also traveled to Vinland, where she set up a trading partnership with two Norse brothers, Helgi and Finnbogi. She double-crossed her partners, however, and had them murdered along with their families.

The legendary Leif

When Freydis returned, Leif did not have the heart to punish her, so he allowed her to go free. By that time, he had settled into his rule as leader of the colony in Greenland, and he never sailed westward again. Nor did any of the other Vikings, but their legends were recorded in *Erik the Red's Saga* and other epic poems describing their voyages.

For many centuries, historians regarded these tales as merely fanciful stories, but in the 1900s evidence began to mount that indeed Norsemen had landed in the New World half a millennium before Columbus. In the 1960s, nearly a thousand years after the founding of Leifrsbudir, archaeologists found remains of a Norse settlement in Newfoundland.

For More Information

Books

Craig, Clare. *Explorers and Traders*. Alexandria, VA: Time-Life Books, 1996.

Grant, Neil. *Eric the Red: The Viking Adventurer.* Illustrated by Victor Ambrus. New York: Oxford University Press, 1998.

Hale, John R. *Age of Exploration.* New York: Time-Life Books, 1974.

Hunt, Jonathan. *Leif's Saga: A Viking Tale.* New York: Simon & Schuster Books for Young Readers, 1996.

January, Brendan. *Explorers of North America.* New York: Children's Press, 2000.

Web Sites

Discoverers Web. [Online] Available http://www.win.tue.nl/~engels/discovery/index.html (last accessed July 26, 2000).

Explorers of the World. [Online] Available http://www.bham.wednet.edu/explore.htm (last accessed July 26, 2000).

The Viking Network Web. [Online] Available http://viking.no/ (last accessed July 26, 2000).

Moses Maimonides

Born 1135
Died 1204

Jewish philosopher

The philosopher Moses Maimonides wrote about a number of subjects, and became justifiably recognized as a man of wisdom not only in spiritual but in scientific matters. As a scholar of the scriptures, he added immeasurably to the literature of the Jewish faith. As a student of philosophy, he achieved a synthesis, or joining, of the ancient Greeks' wisdom with the faith of the Old Testament. As a physician and scientist, he may be considered one of the earliest fathers of psychology as a discipline.

The second Moses

He is known to much of the world as Maimonides (my-MAHN-i-deez), and some scholars of Jewish thought refer to him by the nickname Rambam, but during his lifetime he went by the name Moses ben Maimon (my-MOHN). In Hebrew, *ben* means "son of," and Maimonides's father Maimon was a well-known scholar of the Jewish scriptures. Those scriptures include the Old Testament, and particularly its first five books, known as the Torah. To these, extensive books of

"When speaking, [a scholar] will not raise his voice unduly. His speech with all men will be gentle.... He will judge everyone favorably; he will dwell on the merits of others, and never speak disparagingly of anybody."

Mishneh Torah

Portrait: *Reproduced by permission of the Corbis Corporation.*

223

commentary were added over the years: the Mishnah and the Gemara, which together constitute the Talmud. Much of Maimonides's writing would be concerned with these books of spiritual wisdom.

As for the name Moses, there were few greater names in Jewish history that Maimon could have given to his boy. At the time when the first Moses led the children of Israel out of slavery in Egypt, as described in the Old Testament Book of Exodus, the Israelites celebrated the first Passover, a highly important festival in the Jewish calendar. The "second Moses," as Maimonides came to be called, was born on the eve of Passover, March 30, 1135, which also happened to fall on a Saturday, the Jewish Sabbath, or holy day. To Maimon, all these facts seemed significant, a sign that his son was destined for greatness.

Life in Córdoba

The Jews had long been scattered from their homeland in Palestine, and many, like Maimonides's family, had settled in Spain. The latter was controlled by Muslims, who established a number of flourishing cultural centers such as Córdoba, where Maimonides was born. There Maimonides had an opportunity to interact with people from a variety of cultures, and by interacting with others he supplemented the learning he gained at home and in his father's library.

As a child, Maimonides was a serious-minded boy with a strong sense that he had a mission in life. Therefore he spent little time playing, and devoted much of his attention to educating his younger brother David. When he was thirteen, the quiet life of his family was disrupted when the Almohads (AL-moh-hahdz), an extremist Muslim group, seized control of Córdoba. The Almohads were far less tolerant of other religions than the previous Muslim rulers had been, and the years that followed were tense ones. Finally, in 1160, when Maimonides was twenty-five years old, the family moved to the city of Fez in Morocco.

Years of wandering and tragedy

In Fez, Maimon and David built a successful jewelry business while Maimonides continued to devote himself to his studies, particularly of medicine. Once again, the family lived quietly for a time, and once again their peaceful life was shattered—this time by Maimonides himself. In about 1162, he published his first significant work, translated as *Letter Concerning Apostasy*. Apostasy means rejection of a religious faith, and in this case referred to the Jews' rejection of Islam in favor of holding on to their traditions.

Maimonides's work gave comfort to many, and made him an instant celebrity within the Jewish community, but in light of his sudden prominence, the family judged it wise to leave Morocco. In 1165, they moved to Palestine, but after five months they relocated to Alexandria, Egypt. There tragedy struck a double blow: first Maimon died, then David drowned. Maimonides was devastated, particularly by the death of his younger brother, and he later recalled that for a whole year his grief prevented him from moving on with his life.

But he had to move on, especially because now, at the age of thirty, Maimonides had the responsibility of supporting David's widow and children. Settling in Cairo, he began to make a living as a physician, and he continued his studies. At some point he had married, but his first wife died. Soon afterward, he remarried and had two children, a girl and a boy. The son, Abraham, would later follow in Maimonides's footsteps as a leader in Cairo's Jewish community—as would ten more generations of his family.

The writings of Maimonides

Despite the wide-ranging nature of his scholarly pursuits, Maimonides used a consistent approach to all subjects: first he would study an array of concepts and information, then he would work to bring together all this knowledge and spell it out in a clear, easily understandable form. Thus his work has continued to remain fresh to readers over the centuries.

His principal writings on religious thought were *The Illumination* (1168) and the *Mishneh Torah,* later translated into English as *The Code of Maimonides.* The first of these books was an attempt to render the complex legal writings of

Avicenna

As Moses ben Maimon became more well known in Europe by the westernized name Maimonides, so the Islamic philosopher and scientist ibn Sina is better known in the West as Avicenna (av-i-SEN-uh; 980–1037). More than 150 years before Maimonides, Avicenna was the first to attempt a synthesis, or joining, of ancient Greek philosophy with the principles of religious faith—in this case, Islam.

Born in what is now Afghanistan, Avicenna displayed an early talent as a student, and at the age of ten had already read the entire Koran (kü-RAHN), the Muslim holy book. His family valued study as well, and engaged in lively discussions regarding a number of subjects. Avicenna gained other useful knowledge from an Indian teacher who exposed him to Indian principles of mathematics, including the numeral zero, first used by Hindu mathematicians.

Still more exposure to learning came from a well-known philosopher who stayed with the family for several years and convinced Avicenna's father to allow the boy to pursue a full-time education. The teenaged Avicenna rapidly mastered difficult texts in the sciences and religious scholarship, and was soon teaching physicians and engaging in discussions of Islamic law with highly trained scholars.

His study of logic, or the system of reasoning and testing conclusions, led him to read Aristotle. This reading initially upset him, because he did not know how to square the teachings of the ancient Greek philosopher with those of the Koran. One day, however, his reading of another Islamic scholar helped him unlock the seeming contradiction, and Avicenna was so overjoyed that he gave alms, or money, to the poor in gratitude.

the Mishnah into a form that average readers could understand, and the *Mishneh Torah* classified the vast knowledge contained in the Talmud.

Maimonides's most important philosophical work was the *Guide of the Perplexed,* in which he analyzed the ideas of the Greek philosopher Aristotle (384–322 B.C.), and reconciled these with Jewish beliefs. Although many Jewish scholars had recognized Aristotle's contributions to knowledge, many had found it hard to accept his ideas because he did not worship the God of the Israelites. Maimonides, however, was able to find much in Aristotle that was relevant to Jews' beliefs about morality and other questions.

Avicenna. *Reproduced by permission of the New York Public Library Picture Collection.*

the Muslim world. He wrote more than a hundred books on a variety of subjects, and had a number of adventures as he went from place to place. Among his writings, the *Canon of Medicine* was particularly important, and became a principal source of medical knowledge both in the Middle East and in Europe for centuries. He also wrote poetry, inventing the *rubáiyát* form later used by Omar Khayyám (see box in Dante Alighieri entry).

Like many Muslims of his time, Avicenna owned slaves, and one of these turned against him when he was in his fifties. Hoping to steal his money, the slave put opium, a dangerous drug, into Avicenna's food; but with his knowledge of medicine, Avicenna was able to treat himself and recover. The drug overdose weakened him, however, and in 1037 he had a relapse and died.

Over the years that followed, Avicenna held a number of positions, primarily in the courts of various sultans and emirs, the equivalent of kings and dukes in

Continued influence

In his discussions on the nature of man in the *Guide of the Perplexed,* Maimonides bridged the subjects of philosophy and medicine in an approach that formed the basics of psychology, the study of the human mind. He also wrote directly on the subject of medicine in a number of other works.

Through such writings, Maimonides exerted an influence on thought that continued long after his death in 1204. This influence was not limited to Jewish thinkers, but to the world of scholars in general. Along with Arab writers such as Avicenna (see box) and **Averroës** (see entry), he helped open Christian Europeans' minds to the possibilities of bringing together the principles of religious faith with those of scientific study.

For More Information

Books

Bacon, Brenda, editor. *Rambam: His Thought and His Times.* Drawings by Ida Huberman and Nina Woldin, photography by Suzanne Kaufman. New York: Melton Research Center of the Jewish Theological Seminary, 1995.

Marcus, Rebecca B. *Moses Maimonides: Rabbi, Philosopher, and Physician.* New York: F. Watts, 1969.

Shulman, Yaacov Dovid. *The Rambam: The Story of Rabbi Moshe ben Maimon.* New York: C.I.S. Publishers, 1994.

Web Sites

"Avicenna." [Online] Available http://www-groups.cs.st-and.ac.uk/~history/Mathematicians/Avicenna.html (last accessed July 26, 2000).

"IBN SINA." [Online] Available http://www.mala.bc.ca/~mcneil/sinat.htm (last accessed July 26, 2000).

"Maimon.doc." [Online] Available http://spectrum.net/dede/maimon.htm (last accessed July 26, 2000).

"Maimonides Home Page." [Online] Available http://members.tripod.com/paulmaimon/maimonides.html (last accessed July 26, 2000).

"Moses Maimonides' 'Mishneh Torah.'" [Online] Available http://www.acs.ucalgary.ca/~elsegal/TalmudMap/Maimonides.html (last accessed July 26, 2000).

Mansa Musa

Born c. 1280
Died c. 1337

Emperor of Mali

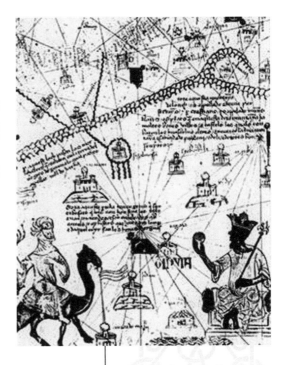

M ansa Musa, emperor of Mali in West Africa, was the first African ruler to become widely known throughout Europe and the Middle East. His was an extraordinarily wealthy land, and it enjoyed respect far and wide, while at home he oversaw a growing and highly organized realm. A devout Muslim, he helped extend the influence of Islam throughout his region, and became celebrated for his pilgrimage to the Muslim holy city of Mecca, during which he stopped in the Egyptian capital of Cairo and spent so much gold that he nearly wrecked the Egyptian economy.

The empire of Mali

The modern nation called Mali (MAH-lee) is a land-locked country which, like much of Africa, suffers under extreme poverty. In the 1990s, the average yearly income there was about the same as the average *weekly* income in the United States. But the medieval empire of Mali was quite a different place. For one thing, it lay along the Atlantic coast, to the

"'This man,' el Mehmendar also told me, 'spread upon Cairo the flood of his generosity: there was no person ... who did not receive a sum of gold from him. The people of Cairo earned incalculable sums from him.... So much gold was current in Cairo that it ruined the value of the money.'"

Al Omari, Egyptian historian

Portrait: Mansa Musa, lower right corner of map.
Reproduced by permission of the Granger Collection Ltd.

southwest of present-day Mali; and more important, it was incredibly wealthy.

The source of Mali's wealth, like that of Ghana (GAH-nuh), an earlier kingdom in the region, was gold. The kings of Ghana had exerted tight control over the gold supply, and the dynasty or royal line that ruled Mali was similarly strong. The founder of this dynasty was Sundiata Keita (sun-JAH-tah kah-EE-tuh; see box in Basil II entry), who established his power through a series of conquests that began in about 1235.

Muslim influence

Mansa Musa—"Mansa" was a title equivalent to *highness*—was either the grandson or the grandnephew of Sundiata, and became Mali's ninth ruler in about 1307. As for his early life, little is known, though it appears likely that he was educated in the Muslim religion.

Islam had taken hold in Mali around 1000, but historians disagree as to whether Sundiata was a Muslim or not. As for Musa, he later became famous for his devotion to the faith. Like many Muslims, he would undertake the *hajj* (HAHJ), the ritual journey to the Islamic holy city of Mecca in Arabia, a duty for all Muslims who can afford to do so. He was apparently the third Malian ruler to do so.

Musa's devotion to Islam put him at odds with groups in Mali who maintained the traditional African religions. Those religions were pagan, meaning that they involved many gods, most of whom had some connection with nature (for instance, a sun god). The conflict between Islam and traditional religions was a serious one, and had helped lead to the downfall of Ghana, whose kings had tried and failed to bring the two religions together.

A strong empire

For the most part, however, Musa was able to avoid serious conflicts over religion, primarily because he was a strong ruler and an effective administrator. His armies were constantly active, extending the power of Mali throughout the region. Even while he was away on his pilgrimage to

Harsha

Like Mansa Musa, the Indian ruler Harsha (c. 590–647) built a great empire in which the arts and culture flourished. Harsha was similarly committed to a religion that placed him in conflict with other groups around him, and as with Musa's Malian empire, the vast realm controlled by Harsha did not long outlast him.

Fifty years before Harsha's time, the Gupta Empire of India had fallen, just as the Western Roman Empire had fallen before it, and in part from the same cause: an invasion by the Huns. In the aftermath, India was ruled primarily by rajas or princes such as Harsha's father, who controlled a small kingdom in the northwestern part of the country.

Harsha did not intend to become a ruler, but a series of misfortunes in his family forced him into action. First his father died; then his mother committed *suttee* (ritual suicide of a widow, a tradition in India); his brother and brother-in-law were murdered; and his sister was placed in danger. Eager for revenge against his brother's mur-

derer, Sanaska (whom he never caught), sixteen-year-old Harsha began a war of conquest that would occupy most of his career.

Over the course of thirty years, Harsha subdued the northern portion of India, the river valleys where most of its people lived. Despite the fact that he was a warrior, he had a great deal of compassion for the poor, an outgrowth of his strong Buddhist faith. The latter placed him in conflict with adherents of the majority Hindu religion, but won him many admirers as well, including the Chinese traveler Hsüan-tsang (shooy-AHND ZAHNG; 602–664). The latter's writings are the principal source of information regarding Harsha's career.

In addition to his skills as a conqueror and ruler, Harsha was also an accomplished playwright. Among his plays was *Priyadarsika,* a clever work using the play-within-a-play structure. Harsha's final play, *Nágánanda* (translated as *The Joy of the Snake-World*), explores Buddhist and Hindu themes.

Mecca, they captured a stronghold of the powerful Songhai (SAWNG-hy) nation to the east. Eventually his empire would control some 40 million people—a population two-fifths the size of Europe at the time—over a vast region nearly the size of the United States.

The power of Mali was partly a result of Musa's strong leadership, but undergirding his power was the wealth of the

A woman walks past a mosque in modern-day Timbuktu, Mali, a country marked by extreme poverty. Under Mansa Musa's rule, the empire of Mali was wealthy and powerful. *Reproduced by permission of the Corbis Corporation.*

nation's gold. That wealth in turn owed something to events far away. For many centuries following the fall of the Western Roman Empire in 476, Europe's economy had been weak; but beginning in about 1100—in part as a result of the Crusades, a series of wars against the Muslims for control of the Middle East—the European economy had begun growing again. This growth created a need for gold coins, which drove up gold prices and in turn increased Mali's wealth. Like the rulers of Ghana before them, the dynasty of Sundiata Keita established a monopoly, or state control, over the gold supply.

Gold wealth in turn spurred cultural advances under Musa's reign. Upon his return from Mecca, Musa brought with him an Arab architect who designed numerous mosques, Muslim places of worship, as well as other public buildings. Some of those mosques still stand in present-day Mali.

Musa also encouraged the arts and education, and under his leadership, the fabled city of Timbuktu became a renowned center of learning. Professors came from as far away as Egypt to teach in the schools of Timbuktu, but were often so impressed by the learning of the scholars there that they remained as students. It was said that of the many items sold in the vast market at Timbuktu, none was more valuable than books.

The pilgrimage to Mecca

In 1324, Musa embarked on his famous pilgrimage to Mecca, on which he was attended by thousands of advisors and servants dressed in splendid garments, riding animals adorned with gold ornaments. He stopped in Cairo, the leading city of Egypt, and spent so much gold that he caused an oversupply of the precious metal. As a result, the value of gold plummeted throughout much of the Middle East for several years; thus, as an unintended result of his generosity, Musa nearly caused the collapse of several nations' economies.

Musa died in 1337 (some sources say 1332), and none of his successors proved to be his equal. Later kings found the vast empire difficult to govern, and they were plagued by religious and political conflicts. By the mid-1400s the Songhai, who rejected Islam in favor of their tribal religions, broke away from Mali and established their own highly powerful state.

But even more powerful forces had been awakened far away—yet another unintended result of Musa's display of wealth. Europeans had some idea of the vast gold supplies in Mali, but when rumors from Egypt began spreading westward, this sealed the fate of the African kingdom. Previously, European mapmakers had filled their maps of West Africa with pictures of animals, largely creations of their own imaginations intended to conceal the fact that they really had no idea what was there. But beginning in 1375, maps of West Africa showed Musa seated on a throne of solid gold. Eager to help themselves to the wealth of the distant land, Portuguese sailors began making their way southward. It was the beginning of the end of West Africa's brief flowering.

For More Information

Books

Burns, Khephra. *Mansa Musa: The Lion of Mali.* Illustrated by Leo and Diane Dillon. San Diego: Harcourt Brace, 2000.

Davidson, Basil. *African Civilization Revisited: From Antiquity to Modern Times.* Trenton, NJ: Africa World Press, 1991.

Davidson, Basil. *African Kingdoms.* Alexandria, VA: Time-Life Books, 1978.

McKissack, Pat. *The Royal Kingdoms of Ghana, Mali, and Songhay: Life in Medieval Africa.* New York: Henry Holt, 1994.

Polatnick, Florence T. and Alberta L. Saletan. *Shapers of Africa.* New York: J. Messner, 1969.

Schulberg, Lucille. *Historic India.* New York: Time-Life Books, 1968.

Web Sites

"African Empires Timeline." [Online] Available http://www.cocc.edu/cagatucci/classes/hum211/timelines/htimeline2.htm (last accessed July 26, 2000).

"Mansa Musa in the Electronic Passport." [Online] Available http://www.mrdowling.com/609-mansamusa.html (last accessed July 26, 2000).

"Medieval India 600–1207." [Online] Available http://www.stockton. edu/~gilmorew/consorti/1eindia.htm (last accessed July 26, 2000).

"Teachers' Guide for FOOTSTEPS' *Mansa Musa, King of Mali* Issue, September 1999." [Online] Available http://cobblestonepub.com/pages/ TGFOOTMansa.html (last accessed July 26, 2000).

Mathematicians and Scientists

Aryabhata

Born 476
Died c. 550

**Indian mathematician
and astronomer**

Al-Khwarizmi

Born c. 780
Died c. 850

**Arab mathematician,
astronomer, and geographer**

Al-Razi

Born c. 864
Died c. 925

Arab physician and philosopher

Alhazen

Born 965
Died 1039

**Arab mathematician
and physicist**

Roger Bacon

Born 1213
Died 1292

**English philosopher
and scientist**

In modern times, people are accustomed to thinking of the West—Western Europe and lands such as the United States that have been heavily influenced by Western Europe—as being at the forefront of mathematical and scientific knowledge. This was not always the case, however: during the Middle Ages, the focal point of learning in math and science lay far to the east, in India and the Arab world.

The five biographies that follow illustrate the process whereby knowledge seeped westward, from the Hindu mathematician Aryabhata in the 500s to the English scientist Roger Bacon seven centuries later. In between were many, many scientists, mathematicians, and philosophers in the region that produced perhaps the greatest intellectual achievements during the medieval period: the Middle East. Al-Khwarizmi, al-Razi, and Alhazen—along with Avicenna (see box in Moses Maimonides entry), **Averroës** (see entry), **al-Mas'udi** (see Historians entry), Omar Khayyám (see box in Dante Alighieri entry), al-Idrisi, and Yaqut— were far from the only notable Arab and Persian thinkers: just some of the greatest.

"Praise God the creator who has bestowed upon man the power to discover the significance of numbers. Indeed, reflecting that all things which men need require computation, I discovered that all things involve number.... Moreover I discovered all numbers to be so arranged that they proceed from unity up to ten."

Al-Khwarizmi, Kitab al-jabr wa al-muquabalah

Two Great Byzantines

Much of the driving force behind advances in science during the Middle Ages came from the rediscovery of ancient Greek texts by Arab scientists. During the early part of the medieval era, the writings of Aristotle and others were lost to Western Europe, where learning in general came to a virtual standstill. By contrast, knowledge of the Greek writers remained alive in the Greek-controlled lands of the Byzantine Empire.

One of the greatest Byzantine commentators on science was not even a scientist but a philosopher and theologian who also wrote about grammar—as his name, John the Grammarian or Johannes Philoponus (yoh-HAHN-uhs ful-AHP-uh-nus; c. 490–570), suggests. Johannes challenged the assertion by Aristotle that a physical body will only move as long as something is pushing it. On the contrary, Johannes maintained, a body will keep moving in the absence of friction or opposition. Five centuries later, Avicenna would uphold Johannes's idea; and many centuries after that, the concept would be embodied in one of the laws of motion established by Sir Isaac Newton (1642–1727).

Also important was the surgeon Paul of Aegina (i-JY-nuh; c. 625–c. 690). He was the first to practice obstetrics, the branch of medical science dealing with birth, as a specialty. His writings summed up virtually all that was known about medicine up to his time, and greatly influenced the work of later Arab scientists.

Aryabhata

During the 500s, at a time when Europe was descending into darkness and Arabia had not yet awakened, India had a thriving scientific community at the city of Ujjain (ü-JYN) in the central part of the subcontinent. Yet Aryabhata (ar-yah-BAH-tuh), one of India's greatest mathematicians, came from Pataliputra (pah-tuh-lee-POO-trah) in eastern India. The city, which had served as the capital of the Mauryan Empire centuries before, had long since fallen into ruins. Symbolic of its state of disrepair was the fact that Pataliputra was a center of superstition where priests taught that Earth was flat and that space was filled with invisible and demonic planet-like forms. The persistence of these ideas made the achievements of Aryabhata all the more impressive.

As was typical of Hindu scientists, Aryabhata considered mathematics of secondary importance to astronomy, and most of his achievements in math were in service to his study of the planets. His greatest work, the *Aryabhatiya,* brought together teachings from ancient Greek and Indian astronomers, and contained a number of cutting-edge ideas: for instance, Aryabhata suggested that the reason why the stars and planets seem to move around Earth is that Earth is in fact rotating on its axis, and moving around the Sun. It would be nearly a thousand years before a Western astronomer, Nicolaus Copernicus, recognized the same fact.

Among Aryabhata's mathematical achievements were great advances in trigonometry (the study of triangles and their properties), as well as the principle of inversion. The latter involves starting with a solution and working backward, developing the steps whereby one reached that solution. Perhaps most notable was Aryabhata's use of two vital concepts, the numeral zero and the idea of number position, or decimal place-value (i.e., tens, hundreds, thousands, etc.). These would have enormous impact as they moved westward. Finally, Aryabhata calculated the most accurate number for pi—a figure equal to approximately 3.14, used for finding the area of a circle—up to that point in history.

Al-Khwarizmi

The word *algebra* is just one of the legacies given to the world of mathematics by al-Khwarizmi (KWAR-iz-mee), a mathematician in the city of Baghdad (now capital of Iraq) who wrote *Kitab al-jabr wa al-muquabalah.* The English name for algebra, a branch of mathematics used for determining unknown quantities, is taken from the second word of the book's title.

Al-Khwarizmi was not only interested in mathematics as an abstract study, but for its practical application; thus one of the principal uses for algebra, as described in his book, was for helping men divide up their inheritances proportionately. In assessing business transactions from a mathematical standpoint, al-Khwarizmi maintained that these transactions involved "two ideas," quantity and cost, and "four numbers"— unit of measure, price per unit, the quantity the buyer wants to purchase, and the total cost.

As with Aryabhata, al-Khwarizmi and his readers considered mathematics merely as a tool in service to other things, including astronomy. The latter was particularly important to Muslims, who needed to know the exact location of the holy city of Mecca, toward which they prayed five times a day. He offered tables and techniques for computing the direction to Mecca and the five times for prayer, which were based on the Sun's position.

Al-Khwarizmi's ideas would prove perhaps even more influential in the West than in the Middle East. A testament to his impact is the word *algorithm,* a term derived from his name and referring to any kind of regularly recurring mathematical operation such as those routinely performed by a computer. One modern scholar maintained that al-Khwarizmi was the single most important mathematician in a fifteen-hundred-year period between about 100 B.C. and the mid-1400s.

Al-Razi

Like al-Khwarizmi, the physician and philosopher al-Razi (RAH-zee), better known in the West as Rhazes (RAHZ-ez), spent much of his career in the great Islamic cultural center of Baghdad. There he wrote a number of important works and established the medieval world's most advanced hospital. In selecting the location for the hospital, it was said that al-Razi had pieces of meat hung in various parts of the city, and picked the place where the meat was slowest to decompose, reasoning that the air was most healthful there. As a doctor he was noted for his compassion, caring for his patient's emotional well-being in addition to their physical bodies, and even helping to support them financially while they recovered at home.

Al-Razi's written works include a ten-volume encyclopedia of medicine as well as a book translated as *Upon the Circumstances Which Turn the Head of Most Men from the Reputable Physician* (c. 919). In it he addressed questions as vital to the medical practice today as they were eleven hundred years ago, warning doctors that patients think they know everything, and encouraging the physicians themselves not to fall under the sway of this mistaken belief. His most important work was *The Comprehensive Book* (c. 930), an encyclopedia in twenty-four volumes that summed up the medical knowledge of his time.

Like many doctors in the premodern period, al-Razi accepted the ancient Greeks' idea that drawing blood would help a patient recover. He did, however, urge caution in doing so, and warned physicians not to apply the technique on the very old, the very young, or the very sick. He applied a variety of herbs and medicines, the uses of which he said he had learned primarily from female healers around the Muslim world.

As both a doctor and a philosopher, al-Razi was interested in alchemy, which was based on the idea that ordinary metals can be turned into precious metals such as gold. Although alchemy was not a real science, it influenced the development of chemistry. Al-Razi's experiments in alchemy may have contributed to his later blindness, and when he died he was in poverty, having given all his wealth to the care of his patients. But he is remembered with great honor: in its School of Medicine, the University of Paris—one of the first institutions of higher education established in the Middle Ages—included the portraits of just two Muslim physicians, al-Razi and Avicenna.

Al-Razi. *Reproduced by permission of the Granger Collection Ltd.*

Alhazen

Born in the city of Basra in what is now Iraq, Alhazen (al-HAHZ-un) achieved fame as a scholar and was invited to undertake a special project in Egypt. The caliph or leader of the Fatimids, an Islamic sect that controlled Egypt in his time, asked him to develop a means for controlling the flooding of the Nile River. Eager for advancement, Alhazen had insisted that he could do so. As he sailed southward on a barge toward the city of Aswan (AHS-wahn), however, he observed the magnificent structures built by the ancient Egyptians, and realized that if the river's flooding could be controlled at all, the people of that great civilization would have managed it thousands of years before. (Only in the 1960s was the Egyptian government, using modern technology, able to construct a dam to deal with this problem.) As for Alhazen, he got out of the job by pretending to be insane, then laid low until the caliph who had hired him died in 1021.

During the remaining eighteen years of his life, Alhazen wrote about a wide array of subjects, most notably optics, or the science of vision. In his day, a number of beliefs about vision prevailed, all of them inherited from ancient times, and all extremely fanciful from the standpoint of modern knowledge. Some theorists promoted the idea of extramission, which maintained that the eye sent out rays that made it possible to see objects. Others claimed intromission, which took a variety of forms but basically came down to the idea that the object sent out rays to the eye. Alhazen was the first to realize that in fact light comes from self-luminous bodies such as the Sun or a lamp, then is reflected off of objects to the eye, which "catches" the reflected rays.

In addition to this and other theories put forth in his most famous work, *Optics,* Alhazen wrote about a number of related subjects such as rainbows, shadows, and the *camera obscura,* an early ancestor of the camera. He also wrote about astronomy, and like a number of Arab thinkers, helped chip away at mistaken beliefs inherited from the Greek astronomer Ptolemy (TAHL-uh-mee; c. A.D. 100–170)—including the idea that other planets revolve around Earth as part of imaginary circles. His greatest achievement, however, was the *Optics,* which influenced Roger Bacon and a number of scientists through Johannes Kepler (1571–1630), the first to add significantly to Alhazen's ideas.

Roger Bacon

Though he wrote widely about a number of scientific disciplines, the greatest contribution of Roger Bacon was in the philosophy of science. Like many Europeans of his day, Bacon, a Franciscan monk from England, was heavily influenced by the scientific knowledge of the Middle East, to which Westerners had first been exposed during the Crusades (1095–1291). Starting in 1247, when he was about thirty-six years old, he became interested in alchemy and other "secret" forms of learning, which he believed would contribute to religious belief.

Many within the Catholic Church, on the other hand, feared that the increase of knowledge in science would damage people's belief in God, and this—combined with the fact that Bacon had a rather disagreeable personality—often got him into trouble. Nonetheless, in 1266 Pope Clement IV took an interest in Bacon's work, and asked for a full report. The result of this request was Bacon's writing of several important works, which unfortunately arrived after the pope's death in November 1266.

Nonetheless, these books have proven highly valuable to scientific knowledge, though not so much for the information they contained as for the principles they outlined. In particular, Bacon helped shape the idea of experimental science, or the gathering and testing of new information.

Roger Bacon. *Reproduced by permission of Archive Photos, Inc.*

For More Information

Books

Bruno, Leonard C. *Math and Mathematicians: The History of Math Discoveries around the World.* Lawrence W. Baker, editor. Detroit: U•X•L, 1999.

Bruno, Leonard C. *Science and Technology Breakthroughs: From the Wheel to the World Wide Web.* Detroit: U•X•L, 1998.

Hoyt, Edwin Palmer. *Arab Science: Discoveries and Contributions.* Nashville, TN: Thomas Nelson, 1975.

The New Book of Popular Science. Danbury, CT: Grolier, 2000.

Stewart, Melissa. *Science in Ancient India.* New York: Franklin Watts, 1999.

Web Sites

"Index of Biographies" (Mathematicians). [Online] Available http://www-groups.dcs.st-andrews.ac.uk/%7Ehistory/BiogIndex.html (last accessed July 26, 2000).

Medieval Technology Pages [Online] Available http://scholar.chem.nyu. edu/technology.html (last accessed July 26, 2000).

Muslim Scientists and Islamic Civilization. [Online] Available http://users. erols.com/zenithco/index.html (last accessed July 26, 2000).

Mohammed I Askia

Born c. 1442
Died 1538

Songhai emperor

Mohammed I Askia ruled Songhai, perhaps the most powerful empire of premodern Africa, at its height. Under his reign, the Songhai controlled a vast area in the continent's western corner, ranging from the dry sands of the Sahara to the dense rain forests of modern-day Nigeria. A devout Muslim, he united much of his land under the faith, and ruled a well-administered empire. In spite of all his achievements, however, he was doomed to die in humiliation, and the empire did not long outlast him.

The Songhai

Though he ruled by the name Mohammed I Askia (ahs-KEE-uh), the latter being the title of the dynasty or royal house he established, he was born Muhammed Ture ibn Abi Bakr (TOOR-ay eeb'n ah-BEE BAHK'r) in about 1442. By that time, Europe was coming out of the Middle Ages, but the modern era would not come to Africa for a few more years—and when it did, it would come in the form of slave-traders dealing in human lives.

"This king makes war only upon neighboring enemies and upon those who do not want to pay him tribute. When he has gained a victory, he has all of them—even the children—sold in the market at Timbuktu."

Leo Africanus, describing Mohammed I Askia

The West Africa of Mohammed's time already knew slavery, and in fact his conquests would bring many new slaves and forced laborers into his empire. This enslavement of Africans by other Africans, of course, lacked the racial overtones that would taint slavery under the Europeans; but there was a distinctly *tribal* and national character to African-upon-African slavery. In West Africa, tribe and nation meant everything, a fact that made the achievements of the Songhai (SAWNG-hy) in building a broad multi-national empire all the more impressive.

The Songhai Empire was centered on the town of Gao (GOW), which lay along a bend in the Niger (NY-jur) River. Gao had existed since about 1000, and the Songhai nation that grew up around it eventually became a part of the empire of Mali. The latter declined, however, after the time of its greatest ruler, **Mansa Musa** (see entry). By the mid-1400s, Songhai had its turn at leadership, and its ruler—a ruthless emperor named Sonni Ali (SAW-nee; ruled c. 1464–92)—was determined to make it an even greater power than Mali had been.

Lieutenant to Sonni Ali

Mohammed belonged to the Soninke (saw-NINg-kay) people, a tribe within the larger empire of the Songhai. He came from a long line of military figures who had seen service in the cavalry of the Songhai armies, and his early education probably combined military and religious studies.

At that time, the influence of Islam had spread throughout the region, and Mohammed's family were Muslims. But not everyone accepted Islam: Sonni Ali, for one, scorned what he saw as a foreign religion. Therefore Mohammed must have kept his beliefs a secret to some degree, because he rose through the ranks to become a trusted lieutenant serving directly under the emperor himself.

The growing empire

Mohammed no doubt participated in Sonni Ali's project of empire-building, because throughout his career, Sonni Ali remained active in the expansion of his realms. To his west was the slowly crumbling empire of Mali, and Sonni Ali took advantage of its situation by sending in his troops and conquering its lands, including the famous city of Timbuktu, in 1468.

The conquest of Mali made the Songhai Empire—which, like other great kingdoms of medieval Africa, possessed enormous wealth in gold—even wealthier. Yet it faced grave dangers on all sides as well: to the north, nomads from the Sahara Desert threatened to invade, and to the south, chieftains of the Mossi people tried to resist Songhai rule.

Sonni Ali had a policy of severe cruelty in dealing with enemies, and this engendered resentment in surrounding lands. His hatred of Islam further made him enemies to the west, especially in regions where the people were more closely related ethnically to North Africans than to sub-Saharan groups such as the Songhai.

Taking power

In 1492, before he had reached all his goals of conquest, Sonni Ali died. Powerful men might have wanted to revolt against him, but no one had dared while the powerful ruler Ali was alive; now Mohammed, for one, saw his chance. In April 1493, he joined forces with dissatisfied Muslim leaders and seized the throne from Sonni Ali's son, who he sent into exile. He then established the Askia dynasty, and set about consolidating his rule.

To ensure that no one challenged his claim on power, Mohammed used exile and even execution to remove members of earlier Songhai ruling families. He used a "carrot-and-stick" approach, applying the "stick" (punishment) to potential rivals for power, and the "carrot" (reward) to Muslim leaders whose favor he wanted to ensure. In the case of the Muslims, who were mostly spiritual and intellectual rather than political leaders, he spent a great deal of money building mosques, or temples, and doing other deeds to win their support.

Strengthening Islamic ties

Mohammed's interest in Islam was not purely that of a believer: he also recognized that the faith, with its simple

Charles the Bold

Duke Charles the Bold (1433–1477) lived at roughly the same time as Mohammed I Askia, though for less than half as long. Both men ruled lands at the height of their power, and both had great ambitions. Both were destined to see those ambitions thwarted, and both died in disgrace.

Burgundy comprised what is now the Netherlands, Luxembourg, and parts of northern France and Belgium. Though it took its name from the Burgundians, a tribe that had conquered the area nearly a thousand years before, its identity as a region went back to the Treaty of Verdun in 843. The latter had divided lands belonging to Charlemagne among three grandsons. One received what became known as the East Frankish Empire, roughly the same as Germany; another took the West Frankish Empire, including most of France; and the third, Lothar, got a strip of land running from the modern-day Netherlands to northern Italy. Though the two Frankish empires survived for some time, the "middle kingdom" of Lotharingia quickly dissolved. It was Charles's dream to rebuild Lotharingia (loh-thar-IN-jee-uh), with Burgundy as its leading power.

Charles's father, Philip the Good, had been an exceedingly popular leader. Charles, however, was moody and egotistical, with a fatal habit of refusing to listen to good advice. On the other hand, he gathered around himself a court noted throughout Europe for its artistic refinement, and he is famous for the financial support he gave to a number of the greatest painters, historians, and musicians of the day.

But politics and war remained the central preoccupations of Charles's short career. During the 1460s, he struggled with Louis XI, king of France, waging an on-again, off-again war. Late in the decade, he tried to forge an alliance with Holy

message and its tightly organized belief system, could be a strong unifying factor in West Africa's world of many gods and many religions. Furthermore, he appreciated the fact that by aligning himself with the Islamic world, he was tapping into a vast civilization stretching from Morocco to western India. What most impressed him was the commercial network of the Muslim world: his empire might possess gold, but without the horses and other goods it could purchase from the other side of the Sahara, his wealth was worthless.

Just as Mansa Musa had done about 175 years before, Mohammed in late 1496 went on a *hajj,* or pilgrimage to

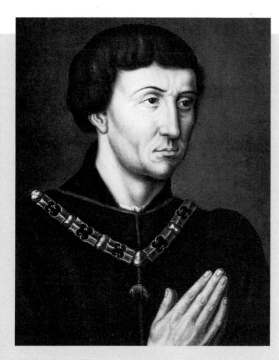

Charles the Bold. *Reproduced by permission of the Corbis Corporation.*

and Lorraine, regions on the border between France and Germany. This frightened the Swiss, whose lands adjoined the area. Louis took advantage of these fears to form an alliance with Switzerland, Austria, and several other local powers against Burgundy.

The two sides met in a series of battles, culminating at Nancy (nahn-SEE) on January 5, 1477. In the Battle of Nancy, Charles was thrown from his horse, and it was several days before gravediggers found his body. Because he had been stripped of his jewels, weapons, and even his clothes, it took some time to identify the corpse as that of Charles the Bold.

After Charles's death, Burgundy was incorporated into France, which by then had become the dominant power on the European continent. One outgrowth of Charles's wars was growing dissatisfaction in the Netherlands, which would declare its independence during the 1600s.

Roman emperor Frederick III, but the emperor politely shunned his advances.

Determined to build his greater Burgundian state between France and Germany, Charles moved his forces into Alsace (al-SAS)

Mecca, as is required of all Muslims who can afford to do so. Highly conscious of the strong impression the Malian emperor had made before him, in particular by spending lavish amounts of gold in Egypt, he made an effort to surpass what Mansa had done. Giving alms to the poor was, like the pilgrimage to Mecca, a duty of all Muslims, and Mohammed was exceedingly generous in his gifts to the poor of Cairo, Egypt's capital city. He also paid to establish and maintain a hostel, a place where pilgrims from West Africa could stay on future pilgrimages.

Again like Mansa Musa, Mohammed attracted considerable attention in the east, where the caliph or ruler of Egypt gave him the title "Caliph of the Blacks." On his return trip, he brought with him a great number of scholars and other esteemed figures from the Arab world, drawn by curiosity and the commanding presence of the African king. These learned men strengthened the already healthy intellectual community of Timbuktu. Around the same time, Djenné (jen-AY), a town on the Niger floodplain to the west, also emerged as a major cultural center.

Widening his kingdoms

The fact that Mohammed stayed away on his hajj for almost two years indicates that he held a firm grip on power. Upon his return, he further strengthened that power with wars of conquest—conflicts which, in the atmosphere of spiritual fervor generated by his trip to Mecca, took on the aspect of *jihad* or holy war for Islam.

Mohammed's armies marched against Mossi tribes to the south, in what is now Burkina Faso. They also moved northward, capturing most of the important Saharan oases and salt mines—the equivalent of islands in a sea of sand—up to the edges of what is now Algeria and Libya. To the east, they conquered powerful Hausa (HOW-suh) city-states in the region of modern-day Nigeria.

Not surprisingly, given his background—not to mention the geographical demands of his large realm, which required mobility—Mohammed's army relied heavily on its cavalry. But his military, perhaps the first standing, or full-time, force in African history, also possessed something unknown in Africa before: a navy, made up of boats that patrolled the Niger.

Glory and exile

Mohammed's Songhai Empire was probably the largest political unit in premodern African history. It possessed a vast military and civilian labor force made up partly of captured peoples, and in later years this force included brigades of slaves detailed to specific jobs such as producing weapons or armor, or fishing to feed the court.

Despite the strength of his empire, Mohammed himself lost his grip on power in 1528. By then he was an old man, more than eighty years of age—exceptionally old for that era—and blind. His son Musa overthrew him, and exiled him to an island in the Niger. Nine years later, another son brought him back from exile to Gao, where he died at about the age of ninety-six.

The Askia dynasty continued to flourish for about a quarter-century after Mohammed's death, and carried on a trading relationship with the distant Ottoman Empire. But changes were coming, particularly with the expansion of European slave-trading activity on the coasts to the south and west. None of Mohammed's successors proved as successful a ruler as he, and religious conflict between Muslim and traditionalist groups further weakened Askia power. In 1561, invaders from Morocco destroyed the Songhai Empire.

For More Information

Books

Adeleke, Tunde. *Songhay*. New York: Rosen Publishing Group, 1996.

Chu, Daniel. *The Glorious Age in Africa: The Story of Three Great African Empires*. Illustrated by Moneta Barnett. Trenton, NJ: Africa World Press, 1992.

Conrad, David C. *The Songhay Empire*. New York: Franklin Watts, 1998.

Koslow, Philip. *Songhay: The Empire Builders*. New York: Chelsea House Publishers, 1995.

Web Sites

"African American Journey: The Songhai Empire." *Worldbook Encyclopedia*. [Online] Available http://www.worldbook.com/fun/aajourny/html/bh016.html (last accessed July 26, 2000).

"African Empires Timeline." [Online] Available http://www.cocc.edu/cagatucci/classes/hum211/timelines/htimeline2.htm (last accessed July 26, 2000).

Medieval Africa. [Online] Available http://historymedren.about.com/education/history/historymedren/msubafr.htm (last accessed July 26, 2000).

Montezuma I

Born 1398
Died 1469

Aztec emperor

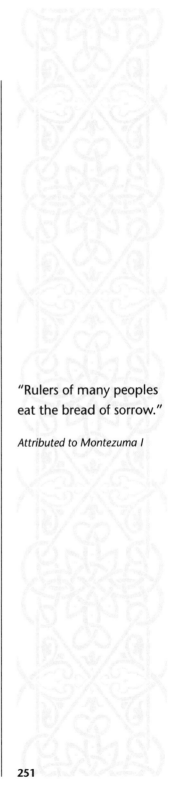

Because the United States borders on Mexico and Americans are relatively familiar with its culture, the name of the Aztec emperor Montezuma is practically a household word. However, that name is typically used in reference to Montezuma II, who ruled from 1502 to 1520 and whose reign was cut short by the arrival of the Spaniards under Hernán Cortés. But before Montezuma II, there were two centuries of Aztec rulers—including the first Montezuma, whose reign ended when Montezuma II was just two years old.

Whereas Montezuma II lived to see defeat at the hands of the invaders, predecessors such as Montezuma I lived and died in a prosperous, powerful empire. The reign of Montezuma I saw its share of troubles, but until the Europeans came, no force was great enough to dislodge the mighty Aztecs.

"Rulers of many peoples eat the bread of sorrow."

Attributed to Montezuma I

The Aztecs

The people known as the Aztecs arrived in central Mexico in about 1250. According to later legends, their priests had been told by the gods that they should claim a spot on the marshy western edge of Lake Texcoco (tays-KOH-koh), today the site of Mexico's capital, Mexico City. Even the name "Mexico" comes from the Aztecs, who called themselves "Mexica" (may-SHEE-kah).

Because of the cruel defeat they later suffered at the hands of the Europeans, it is easy for modern people to believe that the Aztecs themselves were gentle, peace-loving people. Nothing could be further from the truth: in fact, if they had possessed the same level of military technology as the Spaniards, it might well have been the Aztecs who emerged victorious. They were a proud, fierce people whose religion was based on human sacrifice and who exerted their influence through conquests so cruel that their enemies later welcomed the arrival of the Europeans.

But it all started with the tiny settlement on Lake Texcoco, which by 1325 had grown into a great city named Tenochtitlán (tay-nawch-teet-LAHN). The latter would grow in wealth, largely through conquest of neighboring peoples. Military victory also brought in new victims for sacrifice to Aztec gods such as Huitzilopochtli (hwit-zil-oh-POHCH-t'lee) and Quetzalcóatl (kwet-zuhl-KWAH-tuhl). The Aztecs did not only sacrifice enemies, however: Aztec warriors considered it an honor to be chosen as a sacrifice to the gods. Given this fact, it not hard to imagine how formidable Aztec troops were in battle.

"He Who Grows Angry from within His Stomach"

Rulers such as Montezuma I (sometimes rendered as Moctezuma) came from the Aztec nobility, but they also had to be elected. Upon assuming the throne, they were given titles that signified their power: "Prince of the House," "Butcher of Men," "He Who Claws Shedding Blood," and "Lord of the House of Darkness." Montezuma's own name meant "He Who Grows Angry from within His Stomach."

Born in 1398, Montezuma took the throne in 1440, when he was forty-two years old. By that time, the Aztecs had long since set themselves apart from the local tribes, establishing an empire and forming an alliance with two neighboring city-states. Within this triple alliance, however, it was clear that the Aztecs held the true power, and under Montezuma's rule, the empire would expand greatly.

Wars and disasters

Montezuma began by consolidating the gains of his predecessor, Itzcoatl (eest-KWAH-tul; ruled 1427–40), the first to establish full Aztec control over the Valley of Mexico. In 1445, Montezuma led the Aztecs in their conquest of Oaxaca (wah-HAHK-uh), a state that had existed for centuries.

Montezuma's reign was fraught with natural disasters. In 1446, an attack of locusts, a grasshopper-like pest, destroyed most of the crops in the Valley of Mexico. Three years later, Tenochtitlán was flooded. Then in 1450, the region experienced the first of four years of bad harvests caused by drought and early frost.

The famine was so bad, it was said, that people sold themselves into slavery for a few ears of corn. When the cycle of bad harvests ended in 1454, the Aztecs took what they believed was the obvious lesson: the gods had been unhappy because they had not sacrificed enough victims. Therefore the pace of human sacrifices increased dramatically.

Modern-day Mexico City is built on the site where the Aztecs established their first settlement. By 1325 this settlement had grown to be the great city Tenochtitlán.
Reproduced by permission of AP/Wide World Photos.

From sea to sea

From the Zapotec (zuh-POH-tek), founders of Oaxaca, the Aztecs had adopted a dual calendar system, with one calendar based on the 365-day year, and another on a 260-day religious cycle. Once every fifty-two years, the first days of both matched up, and that was a day of celebration for the renewal of the Earth. The year 1455 marked the beginning of a new cycle, and thus despite the misfortunes they had suffered, the Aztecs took heart at what they considered a good sign from heaven.

This Aztec warrior sports a feathered lion's head and a tail. *Reproduced by permission of the Corbis Corporation.*

In 1458, Montezuma led a new series of conquests, expanding the boundaries of the empire so that his people could call themselves "Neighbors of the Sea of the Sky." This referred to their control over lands between the Valley of Mexico and what is today known as the Gulf of Mexico. It is believed that under Montezuma's reign, Aztec territories extended from the Atlantic Ocean to the Pacific.

Doubts about the value of power

Montezuma's court was plagued with the same sorts of intrigues that affected his counterparts in Europe, the Middle East, and East Asia. His half-brother Tlacaelel (t'lah-chay-LEL) may have opposed him for leadership in his early years, though some historians believe he was given an opportunity to take the throne and simply declined. In any case, he was happy to hold power from the sidelines, and after Montezuma's death in 1469, he took control over the empire.

Despite his quest for authority over many lands, Montezuma himself seems to have had doubts about the value of power. Aztec records quote him as saying, "Rulers of many peoples eat the bread of sorrow," and he encouraged his children to seek careers in the trades and crafts, far from the headaches of rulership. Yet after the death of Tlacaelel in 1469, Montezuma's son Axayacatl (ah-say-KAH-tul) took the throne. Just fifty years later, under the reign of Montezuma's namesake Montezuma II, the splendid Aztec Empire came to an end.

For More Information

Books

Bateman, Penny. *Aztecs and Incas: A.D. 1300–1532.* New York: Franklin Watts, 1988.

This painting by the great Mexican painter Diego Rivera (1886–1957) shows the fall of the Aztec Empire to the Europeans. The breakdown of the empire took place under the leadership of Montezuma's namesake, Montezuma II, in 1520. *Reproduced by permission of the Corbis Corporation.*

Chrisp, Peter. *The Aztecs.* Austin, TX: Raintree Steck-Vaughn, 1999.

Gillmore, Francis. *The King Danced in the Marketplace.* Tucson: University of Arizona Press, 1964.

Leonard, Jonathan Norton. *Ancient America.* Alexandria, VA: Time-Life Books, 1967.

Mason, Anthony. *Aztec Times.* New York: Simon & Schuster Books for Young Readers, 1997.

Warburton, Lois. *Aztec Civilization.* San Diego, CA: Lucent Books, 1995.

Wood, Marion. *Growing Up in Aztec Times*. Illustrated by Richard Hook. London: Eagle Books, 1993.

Web Sites

The Aztec. [Online] Available http://northcoast.com/~spdtom/aztec.html (last accessed July 26, 2000).

"The Mexica/Aztecs." [Online] Available http://www.wsu.edu/~dee/ CIVAMRCA/AZTECS.HTM (last accessed July 26, 2000).

Muhammad

Born c. 570
Died 632

Arab prophet, founder of Islam

O nly a handful of people have influenced history as much as the prophet Muhammad. Most of these people were religious teachers such as Jesus Christ, or conquerors such as Alexander the Great. Muhammad, however, was both a religious teacher and a conqueror.

He is often regarded as the founder of Islam, or the Muslim religion, and as the author of its holy book, the Koran. Muslims, however, regard Muhammad as the last in a long line of prophets who brought the truth of Allah, or God, and in their view he did not write the Koran; rather, he received it from Allah. His role as a conqueror is more clear: under his leadership, the Muslim Arabs established the foundations of an empire that would soon rule much of the world.

The world of Muhammad

At the time of Muhammad's birth, few would have suspected that Arabia would soon become the focal point of a great religion and empire. The hot, dry, Arabian Peninsula, an

"There was such sweetness in his visage [appearance] that no one, once in his presence, could leave him. If I hungered, a single look at the Prophet's face dispelled the hunger. Before him all forgot their griefs and pains."

Ali, son-in-law of Muhammad and fourth caliph

Portrait: *Reproduced by permission of the Corbis Corporation.*

257

area about half the size of the United States, offered little to attract outsiders; it was simply a place for goods, carried by camels on caravans, to pass through on their way between Africa, Europe, and Asia.

Arabia was a tribal society, divided between the nomadic Bedouins (BED-oo-unz) of the desert and the settled peoples of the coastal areas. A dominant cultural center was Mecca, located halfway down the coast of the Red Sea that separated Arabia from Africa. Among Mecca's attractions was a shrine called the Kaaba (kuh-BAH), a cube-shaped building that housed a meteorite. The latter, according to the traditions of the Arabs, had been hurled to Earth by a god known as Allah. In addition to Allah were some 300 other gods and goddesses, whose statues filled the Kaaba; yet Allah was supreme, like the God worshiped by Jews and Christians.

The leading tribe of Mecca was called the Quraish (koo-RESH), and it was into this tribe that Muhammad was born. His father Abdullah ("servant of Allah") died a few weeks before Muhammad was born, and his mother Amina died when he was six. Muhammad lived with his grandfather until the latter died when the boy was eight. Thereafter he lived with the family of his uncle Abu Talib, leader of the Hashim clan.

Khadijah

When he was about twenty-five years old, Muhammad went to work for a wealthy widow named Khadijah (kah-DEE-zhah). He soon gained her trust, and she authorized him to act as her representative in a merchant business that took him to Syria. There Muhammad undoubtedly gained exposure to various ideas and traditions, including Judaism and Christianity.

Though Khadijah was nearly fifteen years his senior, Muhammad so impressed her that she proposed marriage. They married, and she bore him many children, of which only four daughters survived. Soon Muhammad was so wealthy that he could afford to take his cousin Ali, son of Abu Talib, into his household. Later Ali would marry Muhammad's daughter Fatima (FAT-uh-muh, "shining one"), the only one of his daughters to bear him grandchildren.

His first revelation

For many years, Muhammad lived the ordinary life of a prosperous merchant; but as he neared the age of forty, he became drawn to Mount Hira outside Mecca, where he spent time meditating. According to Islamic tradition, it was there that the angel Gabriel—mentioned in the Bible—appeared to him one day holding a cloth on which something was written, and demanded of him, "Recite!"

Muhammad asked "What shall I recite?" and Gabriel covered his face with the cloth, so that Muhammad thought he would suffocate. They went through this three times, until finally Gabriel began dictating words to him. This was the first of some 650 revelations, or visions, in which he received the text of the Koran or Quran (kü-RAHN), Islam's holy book.

Naturally, Muhammad doubted what had happened to him, but when he told Khadijah about his experience, she assured him that his revelation must have truly been from God.

An ancient handwritten copy of the Koran, the holy book of Islam. Muslims believe the Koran was received by the prophet Muhammad directly from Allah. *Reproduced by permission of Archive Photos, Inc.*

Thus she became the first convert to the Muslim (MUZ-lim) or Islamic (iz-LAHM-ik) faith. (The word *Islam* in Arabic means "submission to God," and *Muslim* "one who submits to God.")

The growth of Islam

Muhammad's next convert was Ali, followed by a former slave who Muhammad had adopted. The first convert from outside Muhammad's household was Abu Bakr (ah-BOO BAHK-ur), whose daughter Aisha (ah-EE-shah) Muhammad would marry many years later.

The "new" religion—Muslims believe that the truths of Islam are eternal, and existed long before they were revealed to Muhammad—had much in common with Judaism and Christianity. It placed great importance on figures from the Old Testament such as Abraham, father of the Jews, and even on Jesus Christ. But it taught, in the words by which Muslims are called to prayer five times a day throughout the world, that "there is no god but Allah, and Muhammad is his prophet."

This faith had an important social message as well as a religious one: in place of the traditional clan loyalties of the Arab world, it taught that all men are one in the eyes of Allah. This was not a message welcomed by the leaders of Mecca, who saw in it a threat to their power. Soon Muhammad and his followers would face off against the Meccan leaders.

In 619, Khadijah died. Muhammad later took a total of eleven wives and concubines—in some cases to strengthen political ties, in other instances to provide for the widows of followers who had died in battle—but none of them ever assumed the importance of his first love. Around this time, he had a miraculous experience, the only miracle associated with Muhammad other than the revelation of the Koran. It was said that he traveled in a single night from Mecca to Jerusalem, holy city of the Old Testament, and from there ascended into heaven and met with the prophets of old; then he returned to Mecca, all in a single night.

The *hegira*

By 622, relations between the Muslims and the leaders of Mecca had deteriorated badly. Meanwhile the people of

Yathrib (YAH-thrub), an oasis some two hundred miles to the north, invited Muhammad to come lead them. Muhammad sent most of his followers ahead, then escaped from Mecca himself, and arrived in Yathrib on September 24, 622. Henceforth Yathrib would be known as Medina (muh-DEEN-uh; "The City"). Muslims call Muhammad's flight from Mecca the *hegira* (heh-JY-ruh), and date their calendar from this event, just as Christians date theirs from the birth of Christ.

Over the coming years, Muhammad led his followers on several raids against trading caravans from Mecca, and this eventually led to outright warfare between Mecca and Medina. The two forces clashed at the wells of Badr (BAHDr), and though the Muslims were outnumbered three to one, they scored a significant victory. Meanwhile in Medina, Muhammad found himself in conflict with members of the Jewish community, who disputed his claim to have received a true revelation from God. In time Muhammad would become hostile toward certain Jewish groups, though not to Jews as a whole.

In March of 625, Muhammad's army suffered a defeat at the hands of the forces from Mecca, and the Meccan leaders began to grow confident. Two years later, in March of 627, they approached Medina with a large army, but Muhammad's forces dug a trench around part of the city and held off the invasion. Fearing Jewish traitors in the city, Muhammad dealt harshly with some Jews, but allowed those who offered no opposition to continue living among the Muslims and practicing their religion as before.

Conquering Mecca

Another year passed, and in March of 628, Muhammad led a large group to Mecca, not for the purposes of an invasion but to make a pilgrimage, or a visit for religious purposes. They did not gain entrance to the city, but they stayed and negotiated a truce whereby the two sides agreed to maintain peace for ten years.

Soon, however, allies of Mecca broke the truce by attacking the Muslims, and in January of 630, Muhammad set out from Medina with a large army. A number of Mecca's leaders came out to meet him, and pledged their loyalty,

Aerial view of the Great Mosque in Mecca, the holy city of Islam. The shrine called the Kaaba is in the courtyard of the Great Mosque. *Reproduced by permission of the Corbis Corporation.*

whereupon he promised that he would not harm anyone who did not oppose him.

True to his word, upon entering the city he killed only his true enemies, and ordered the destruction of the idols—the statues of the gods—in the Kaaba. Thenceforth Mecca would be the holy city of Islam, so revered that Muslims consider it a sacred duty to visit the city at least once in their lifetimes if they can afford to do so; but Muhammad himself continued to live in Medina.

Muhammad's legacy

Throughout the years of his exile, Muhammad had acted as unofficial leader of Medina, advising those who held political power. An important aspect of Islam was the fact that it addressed not just spiritual matters, but everyday issues, and this, combined with followers' intense devotion to their faith, ensured that the Muslims would bring many lands under their control.

In his last two years, Muhammad concerned himself with subduing nearby communities. He spent much of his time with Aisha, some forty-four years his junior, who became his most important wife after Khadijah. In March of 632, he made a final pilgrimage to Mecca, then returned to Medina in ailing health. On June 8, he died with his head on the lap of Aisha.

There was only one prophet of Islam, and no one could take Muhammad's place after his death; still, the Muslims needed a caliph (KAL-uf), a spiritual and political leader. Muhammad had no son, and in Arab society, it was unthinkable that a woman should lead; therefore the first four caliphs were men connected to the prophet through his wives. The first caliph was Abu Bakr, followed by the father of another wife; then Uthman (üth-MAHN), who married one of Muhammad's childless daughters; and fourth was Ali.

When Muhammad died, the Muslims held only the western portion of Arabia; less than 30 years later, the caliphate stretched from Libya far in the west to Bactria or Afghanistan in the east, and from the Caspian Sea in the north to the Nile River in the south. But there were also divisions within the ranks, particularly between Aisha on one side, and Ali and Fatima on the other. This would ultimately lead to a split between the majority *Sunni* (SOO-nee) Muslims and the *Shi'ite* (SHEE-ight) Muslims, who claimed that Ali was the only rightful caliph. Nonetheless, Islam spread throughout the known world, and today claims more than 1.14 billion followers—more than any religion other than Christianity.

For More Information

Books

Guillaume, Alfred. *The Life of Muhammad: A Translation of Ibn Ishaq's Sirat Rasul Allah.* New York: Oxford University Press, 1955.

The Muslim Almanac. Detroit: Gale, 1996.

Stewart, Desmond and the Editors of Time-Life Books. *Early Islam.* New York: Time-Life Books, 1967.

Suskind, Richard. *The Sword of the Prophet: The Story of the Moslem Empire.* Illustrated by Enrico Arno. New York: Grosset & Dunlap, 1971.

Web Sites

"About the Prophet Muhammad (SAAS)." [Online] Available http://www.usc.edu/dept/MSA/fundamentals/prophet/ (last accessed July 26, 2000).

IslamiCity in Cyberspace. [Online] Available http://www.islam.org/ (last accessed July 26, 2000).

"Muhammad (570–632)." [Online] Available http://malvm1.mala.bc.ca/~mcneil/muhammad.htm (last accessed July 26, 2000).

Prophet Muhammad. [Online] Available http://www.muhammad.net (last accessed July 26, 2000).

Murasaki Shikibu

Born c. 978
Died 1026

Japanese author

The writing of novels, extended works of fiction written in prose rather than poetry, is a relatively recent development: Giovanni Boccaccio's *Decameron* (1353; see box), which is considered by some to be one of the first "novels," was not really a novel but a collection of short tales. Among the earliest works typically recognized as novels were *Gargantua and Pantagruel* by François Rabelais of France (c. 1495–1553), *Don Quixote* by Miguel de Cervantes of Spain (1547–1616), and *Pilgrim's Progess* by John Bunyan of England (1628–1688). Yet many centuries before these men, the first novel in history made its appearance. Its author was not a European—nor was she a man.

She was Murasaki Shikibu, author of the *Tale of Genji*. Much about her life is a mystery: historians do not even know her real name. But perhaps the key to her deepest thoughts lies in a character from her strangely engaging tale. That character is not Genji, the lusty hero, but his favorite among his many ladies: a sensitive, gentle soul named Murasaki.

"The priest began to tell stories about the uncertainty of this life and the retributions of the life to come. Genji was appalled to think how heavy his own sins had already been.... But immediately his thoughts strayed to the lovely face which he had seen that afternoon; and longing to know more of her he asked, 'Who lives with you here?'"

Tale of Genji

Giovanni Boccaccio

Prior to the late Middle Ages, writers of tales—for instance, the ancient Greek poet Homer in the *Iliad*—tended to write in verses, whereas later authors would use the prose narrative format familiar to all readers of novels today. In this regard and many others, the work of Giovanni Boccaccio (boh-KAHT-choh; 1313–1375) is significant. His early writing used verse forms, as had the work of his distinguished predecessors **Dante** (see entry) and Petrarch; later, the *Decameron,* by far his most well-known piece, used prose narrative in the form of 100 short tales.

Boccaccio was the illegitimate son of a merchant who legally adopted him and took over his care when he was seven years old. From age fourteen, he lived with his father in Naples, a sunny port city in the south of Italy that to Boccaccio's mind seemed to throb with a spirit of adventure. His father intended him to study banking, but Boccaccio had other interests in mind: one was writing, and another was the opposite sex. As Dante had Beatrice and Petrarch had Laura—in both cases, women the poets hardly knew, but worshiped from afar—Boccaccio had Fiammetta, who in reality may have been the daughter of the king of Naples. It is also possible that Boccaccio, unlike the other two poets, had a genuine relationship with the object of his desire; but it is difficult to separate truth from Boccaccio's romantic tales.

By his early twenties, Boccaccio had already demonstrated great talent as a storyteller. He was only twenty-seven in 1340, when he left Naples for Florence, farther up the Italian peninsula, but he had already completed three extended tales in verse. At first he was not happy in Florence, but as he produced book after book, he established himself as the leading author of his time.

The city of Florence, like much of Europe, was devastated by the Plague, or Black Death (1347–51), which wiped out a huge portion of the population—including Boccaccio's father and stepmother. As painful as the Plague was for him, however, it also resulted in the writing of the *Decameron* (1353). In the latter, a group of seven young women and three young men escaping the Plague flee the city and

The meaning of her name

In early medieval Japan, surnames or family names were uncommon, and often a daughter was identified by the title of her father or another powerful man in her life. *Shikibu* was the title of Murasaki's father, who served in the court of the Japanese emperor. This would be equivalent to a girl being called "doctor" or "lawyer." As for *Murasaki,* which means

Giovanni Boccaccio. *Reproduced by permission of the Library of Congress.*

significance when compared to his many other writings both before and after the 1350s. It appears, however, that Boccaccio sometimes showed poor judgment and had trouble estimating the proper worth of something. He was not always wise in his choice of friends, for instance: he remained impressed with Niccolò Acciaiuoli (aht-chy-WOH-lee), who he had known from his early days in Naples, despite the fact that Acciaiuoli often let him down. The two often quarreled, yet Boccaccio remained dedicated to Acciaiuoli.

Boccaccio also had at least one falling-out with Petrarch, who he first met in September 1350; ultimately, however, the two giants of Italian literature patched up their differences. From the early 1360s, Boccaccio lived quietly in his hometown, Certaldo, where he devoted his time to friends, politics, and literature. Having produced numerous works other than the *Decameron,* including a biography of Dante, Boccaccio died four days before Christmas in 1375.

amuse themselves by telling 100 tales, mostly about love. What sets the *Decameron* apart from much of the literature that preceded it is its natural, everyday tone, which would later have a profound influence on **Geoffrey Chaucer** (see entry on English Scholars, Thinkers, and Writers).

Boccaccio himself seems to have considered the *Decameron* a work of little

"purple," this was a complex pun of a type familiar in China and Japan, which at that time bore a heavy Chinese influence.

Purple is one of the colors of the wisteria flower, whose symbol in the Chinese system of writing made up the first syllable of the name Fujiwara ("wisteria plain.") Fujiwara was the name of the most powerful family in Japan, which since the mid-600s had been the real power behind the imperial throne. Through marriage and other alliances, the Fujiwara—more of an extended clan than a mere family—had made their influence felt far and wide. Murasaki's father, Fujiwara no Tametoki (tahm-uh-TOH-kee) belonged to a minor branch of the powerful clan, and his position as a low-ranking official reflected that fact. Therefore by giving his daughter a name that suggested that of the Fujiwara, Murasaki's father was establishing a subtle link between her and the great family tradition that preceded her.

Early literary talent

The father's rank was low in a relative sense, of course: he was still a part of the imperial court in the capital city of Heian (hay-YAHN; now Kyoto), which gave its name to the period in Japanese history from 794 to 1185. The upper classes of Japan during this time put a high emphasis on cultural refinement, which they equated with a knowledge of Chinese ways. Thus the father, following in the footsteps of his own father and grandfather, built a reputation for himself with his mastery of Chinese philosophy and literature.

Murasaki, too, had a great knowledge of, and appreciation for, the Chinese classics. This knowledge was unusual at a time when girls were expected to learn arts such as embroidery while the men busied themselves with more mentally challenging pursuits. As a matter of fact, Murasaki proved to be better at writing in Chinese than her brother, and she and her father developed a special bond over this shared love. Often she would quote to him from the Chinese histories, or compose poetry in imitation of one Chinese master or another.

The *Tale of Genji*

In 996, when she was about eighteen years old, Murasaki's father took a post as governor of a distant province, and Murasaki went with him. Two years later, however, she returned to Kyoto to marry a man of the Fujiwara clan who was nearly as old as her father. Fujiwara no Nobutaka already had children by other women, and was known as a demanding man, but their marriage seems to have been a happy one. In 999, she gave birth to a daughter, Kenshi, who later grew up to be a poet herself. Soon after the birth of Kenshi, Murasaki's husband died in an epidemic.

No doubt to comfort herself in the face of her loss, Murasaki now returned to her early love of writing. In about 1002, she began work on a story concerning the adventures of a hero named Genji ("the shining one"). This was the beginning of what became *Genji monogatari,* or the *Tale of Genji,* which she completed some two years later.

Murasaki's Genji is the son of an emperor and one of the emperor's lesser wives, and the book is simply the tale of his romantic experiences. From a Western perspective, it does not have a hair-raising plot: Japanese art forms tend to be more subdued than their Western counterparts, and likewise Japanese stage plays seem almost plotless to someone accustomed to the work of William Shakespeare or other European writers.

Yet the *Tale of Genji* is filled with an enormous sense of the deeper meaning in life, and raises questions concerning what is permanent and what is only a part of the passing moment. Though it is a seemingly lighthearted tale of a handsome young man's adventures in love, its bubbly surface conceals much deeper anxieties that plague Genji—anxieties that grow as the story moves toward its conclusion.

The real Murasaki

A thousand years after Murasaki, writers considered themselves clever if they managed to work in some reference to themselves in a story. (For instance, the twentieth-century British humorist P. G. Wodehouse had a character in a story suggest that the only writers worth reading were Leo Tolstoy, author of *War and Peace,* and P. G. Wodehouse.) Readers delighted in such instances of self-reference, just as movie fans have studied the films of Alfred Hitchcock for the director's trademark appearances as a background figure—a man passing by on the street, for instance—in his own films.

In fact this use of self-reference is an old technique, perhaps first pioneered in Murasaki's use of the character "Murasaki" in the *Tale of Genji.* Murasaki is a comforting presence, a gentle and sensitive figure who offers peace to the restless Genji. Perhaps this was a revelation of Murasaki's inner self; certainly her diary and autobiographical writings, composed after she joined the imperial court in 1005 as a companion to the emperor's young wife, reveal little about her real feelings.

In the Japanese culture of the Middle Ages, it was considered inappropriate for anyone to share their innermost thoughts with others, and this was doubly so for a woman of the upper classes. But Murasaki seems to have been even more reserved than most, because in her diary she remarked that other women of the palace resented her distant manner. She confessed through words delivered from Genji's mouth that she wrote because she "was moved by things, both good and bad," and wanted to "make [them] known to other people—even to those of later generations."

Little is known about who Murasaki was in life, and still less is known about how her life ended. It is possible that she left the court to become a Buddhist nun, and spent her final years in quiet contemplation. Some records indicate that she died in her thirties, others in her late forties. She is believed to be buried in Kyoto, but historians are unsure of her grave site's exact location.

For More Information

Books

Encyclopedia of World Biography, second edition. Detroit: Gale, 1998.

Reference Guide to World Literature, second edition. Detroit: St. James Press, 1995.

Uglow, Jennifer S., editor. *The Continuum Dictionary of Women's Biography.* New York: Continuum Publishing, 1989.

Women's Firsts. Detroit: Gale, 1997.

Web Sites

Barrick, Christine. "Giovanni Boccaccio." [Online] Available http://www.phs.princeton.k12.oh.us/Public/Lessons/enl/barr.html (last accessed July 26, 2000).

"Boccaccio and Decameron: Guide to Websites." [Online] Available http://www.sfu.ca/~finley/decaguide.html (last accessed July 26, 2000).

"Female Heroes: Murasaki Shikibu." *Women in World History.* [Online] Available http://www.womeninworldhistory.com/heroine9.html (last accessed July 26, 2000).

"Genji on the Web (Watson)." [Online] Available http://www.meiji-gakuin.ac.jp/~watson/genji/genji.html (last accessed July 26, 2000).

"Giovanni Boccaccio, 1313–1375." [Online] Available http://www.pagesz.net/~stevek/ancient/boccaccio.html (last accessed July 26, 2000).

Hines, Sarah. "Lady Murasaki's The Tale of Genji." [Online] Available http://www.sla.purdue.edu/academic/fll/Japanese/JPNS280/projects/Hines.htm (last accessed July 26, 2000).

"Murasaki Shikibu: Japan's First Novelist." [Online] Available http://picpal.com/genji.html (last accessed July 26, 2000).

"Shikibu Murasaki Q & A." [Online] Available http://www4.justnet.ne.jp/~cosmotown/shikibu/oshiete-e.html (last accessed July 26, 2000).

Osman I

Born 1259
Died 1326

Turkish warlord, founder of Ottoman Empire

Today Istanbul is a magnificent city that serves as a crossroads between worlds: Europe, of which it is geographically a part, and the Asian mainland of Turkey just a few miles distant, to which it is culturally tied by nearly six centuries of history. Once, however, Istanbul was Constantinople, capital of the Byzantine Empire, and its fall to the Ottoman Turks in 1453 was regarded as a crisis for the Christian nations of Europe.

The fall of Constantinople was one of the events that heralded the end of the Middle Ages, but it had been foreseen nearly two centuries before—according to legend, at least—in a dream by Osman I, founder of the Ottoman Empire. It is no wonder that such a leader, who founded one of the world's longest-lasting empires, would inspire many legends; however, the reality of Osman's life was remarkable enough.

Roots of the Turks

Until the eleventh century, Asia Minor, or Anatolia, site of modern-day Turkey, was primarily inhabited by peo-

"That city [Constantinople], placed at the juncture of two seas and two continents, seemed like a diamond set between two sapphires and two emeralds, to form the most precious stone in a ring of universal empire. Othman [Osman] thought that he was in the act of placing that visioned ring on his finger, when he awoke."

Edward S. Creasy, History of the Ottoman Turks

Portrait.

273

Balkan Heroes

The Balkan Peninsula, the southeastern corner of the European continent, is at the crossroads of many worlds: Roman Catholic and Greek Orthodox, Christian and Muslim, European and Asian, Western and Eastern. Not surprisingly, then, it has been the site of numerous conflicts.

In the twentieth century, World War I began in what is now Bosnia, and World War II saw heavy fighting throughout the area. The postwar years were a time of intense hatred and suppressed conflict in the Communist nations of the Balkans, and the years since the fall of Communism have produced ethnic wars involving Serbia and its neighbors. The Middle Ages were no different, with wars involving the Ottoman Turks and other forces. Along with its wars, however, the era also produced a number of heroes.

One of the earliest was Boris I (ruled 852–89), the Bulgarian ruler who converted his nation to Christianity. Though there were Catholic missionaries in the area, Boris accepted the Greek Orthodox faith, and modeled many aspects of his realm on the Byzantine, or Eastern Roman, Empire. He even adopted the ancient Roman title of "caesar," or *czar* (ZAR). Boris

in fact became so interested in Christianity that he abdicated, or resigned from the throne, and spent most of his last eight years in a monastery. Bulgaria flourished under his successors, briefly becoming a power that overshadowed both the Byzantines and the Russians in the 900s.

Far to the other side of the Balkan Peninsula was Croatia, whose first king was Tomislav in the tenth century. Long before, under the rule of **Charlemagne** (see entry), Croatia had accepted Roman Catholicism rather than Greek Orthodoxy. Tomislav, however, faced an enemy that accepted no form of Christianity: the Magyars, destined to found the nation of Hungary. In fighting back the pagan invaders, Tomislav added considerable territory, and united Croatia for the first time.

To the south of Croatia was Bosnia, where even today, people use the expression "to talk of Ban Kulin," meaning "to speak of better times." This is a reference to Kulin (ruled c. 1180–c. 1204), a *ban*, or local ruler. Despite the fact that Hungary then controlled the area, Ban Kulin helped the tiny nation achieve a measure of independence. A Catholic, he revolted against Rome by becoming a Bogromil, a member

ples with close cultural ties to the Greeks. As for the Turks, who eventually gave the land its name, they came from a broad stretch of Central Asia outside the Chinese borders, from whence they began moving westward in the 500s.

of a Bulgarian sect that asserted God had two sons, Christ and Satan. In 1203, the pope forced Ban Kulin to renounce the Bogromil faith.

Ultimately most Bosnians would become Muslims, since their country, along with much of the Balkan Peninsula, would be annexed to the Ottoman Empire. Before it fell to the Ottomans, however, neighboring Serbia experienced a flowering under a series of kings named Stephen. The greatest of these was Stephen Dusan (dü-SHAHN; 1308–1355), who seized the throne from his father in 1331. He went on to conquer a number of lands from the Byzantines, and in 1346 had himself crowned emperor of the Serbs, Greeks, Bulgars, and Albanians. Four years later, he conquered Bosnia, and was marching on Constantinople in 1355 when he died.

Serbia's dreams would be dashed in a battle at Kosovo—ironically, the site of a modern-day conflict involving Serbia and Albania—in 1389. At Kosovo Field, known as "the field of the black birds," the Ottomans dealt the Serbs under Prince Lazar (1329–1389) a humiliating defeat, and soon afterward added Serbia and Bulgaria to their empires.

Fifty years later, Kosovo was the site of another battle between Ottoman forces and an Eastern European hero, Hungary's János Hunyadi (YAH-nos HOON-yahd-ee; c. 1407–1456). Trained as a knight, Hunyadi scored early victories against the Turks in the 1430s, and even drove the Ottomans out of Serbia, Bosnia, Albania, and Bulgaria. This put the Hungarians in a position to influence the region, but with Hunyadi's defeat by the Turks at Kosovo, those hopes came to an end.

Hunyadi was almost the exact contemporary of Albania's Skanderbeg (1405–1468). The name, given to him by the Turks, is a version of Alexander, and calls to mind Alexander the Great; his real name was George Kastrioti (kahs-tree-OHT-ee). Brought up as a Muslim among the Turks, in his late thirties he became a Christian, abandoning the Turks and supporting the cause of his own people. His defeat of Ottoman forces under the sultan Murad II in 1450 made Skanderbeg a hero throughout Europe; but soon after his death in 1468, Albania became a part of the Ottoman Empire.

Turks settled in various places, but perhaps no group was as notable as the Seljuks, a dynasty founded by Toghril Beg (see box in Shotoku Taishi entry). They defeated the Byzantines at the Battle of Manzikert in 1071, putting that empire's fortunes in a downward spiral from which it would not recover. They also laid claim to Anatolia, which would remain in Turkish hands from then on.

A world of fading empires

Osman (AWS-mahn), who came from the Ghazi (GAHZ-ee) tribe of Turks, was born in 1259. Legend has it that his grandfather led the Ghazis out of northeastern Iran. After the grandfather's death along the way westward, Osman's father Ertogrul (urt-oh-GRÜL) replaced him.

By then the Mongols were on the move, and Ertogrul supported the Seljuks against these invaders. This might have seemed like an obvious choice since the Ghazis and Seljuks were related, but the Seljuks were nonetheless grateful and rewarded Ertogrul for his support by granting him lands in northeastern Anatolia.

Though the Mongols' realms were still growing at that time, the Ghazis were surrounded by fading empires. At one time, the Muslim world had been ruled by the Abbasid caliphate in Baghdad, but its power had been broken by the Seljuks in 1258. Now the power of the Seljuks, too, was in decline. To the west was the Byzantine Empire, whose people adhered to the Greek Orthodox form of Christianity. The Ghazis, on the other hand, were Muslims, and like the Abbasids and the Seljuks before them, they viewed any conflict with the Byzantines as a "holy war" on behalf of their religion. Thus Osman would feel justified in later building his empire at the expense of the Byzantines.

Osman's dream

One of the most powerful legends of Osman's early life concerned a dream in which he saw himself taking the Byzantine capital at Constantinople. That literal dream, and the figurative dream of empire that it spawned, was closely tied with a love affair.

As a youth, Osman reportedly fell in love with Malkhatun (mahl-hkhah-TOON), whose name means "treasure of a woman." He asked her to marry him, but her father, a respected Muslim holy man, refused—no doubt because Osman was a rough chieftain and warlord. Years passed, during which time Osman asked again and again for the hand of Malkhatun, only to be refused each time. Finally he had come to accept the fact that they would never marry; then one night, he had a dream.

In his dream, he was sleeping alongside a friend when a full moon arose from his friend's chest, then floated over to Osman and sank into his own chest. The moon symbolized Malkhatun, and its joining of his chest was their marital union. Then out of Osman's chest grew a great tree, which rose to shadow the entire world. A wind began to blow all the trees' leaves toward Constantinople, which came to resemble a ring. Osman was just about to put the ring on his finger when he awoke.

It is not hard to believe that Osman had this dream of empire; much more difficult to believe is the story that upon hearing of the dream, Malkhatun's father changed his mind and allowed the marriage. Probably the whole tale was created long after Osman's time; whatever the case, he did go on to marry Malkhatun and to found a great empire.

The conquest of Bursa

Out of respect for his Seljuk hosts, Osman's father had not tried to expand his territories. But times were changing: the Mongols had destroyed the Seljuks' power, and when Osman became chieftain in 1288, he set about acquiring new lands. From 1299, when he refused to pay tribute or tax money to the Mongol ruler, he symbolically created his own state, which would form the nucleus of the realm named after him: the Ottoman Empire.

During the period from 1300 to 1308, Osman fought a number of engagements, successively taking pieces of Anatolia from the Byzantines. Finally he reached the city of Bursa, only seventy miles from Constantinople across the Sea of Marmara. Osman would never live to see the conquest of Constantinople, however: his last eighteen years would be caught up in a struggle to take Bursa.

The conquest of the city looked easier than it was. From 1308 Osman's troops controlled almost all areas around it, but it took them another thirteen years to seal off Bursa's port at Mudanya (moo-DAHN-yah). The Byzantines proved stubborn adversaries, and even after the taking of Mudanya, the Turks had to maintain a five-year-long siege against Bursa before the city finally yielded in 1326.

Six centuries of empire

As a major commercial center, Bursa was a huge gain to the Ottoman Turks. Osman himself, however, did not live to enjoy the triumph: when he learned about the city's capture from his son Orkhan (ruled 1326–62), he was on his deathbed. Giving Orkhan some final advice about treating all his subjects equally and fairly, Osman died at the age of sixty-seven.

The empire grew quickly under Osman's successors, and it rapidly acquired much of the Balkan Peninsula on Europe's southeastern tip. Given the weakness of the Byzantines, then, it is surprising that more than 125 years passed between the death of Osman and the taking of Constantinople. However, the Byzantines were fierce in holding on to what remained of their empire, and the invasion of Anatolia by **Tamerlane** (see entry) in about 1400 slowed the Ottoman advance.

By the mid-1400s, however, the Ottomans had won the prize dreamt of long before by Osman. The empire kept growing until 1683, by which time it dominated a huge portion of southeastern Europe, all of the Middle East and North Africa, and much of what is now southern Russia. Thereafter it went into a long decline, just like the Byzantine Empire had long before. It came to an official end only in 1922.

For More Information

Books

Andryszewski, Tricia. *Kosovo: The Splintering of Yugoslavia.* Brookfield, CT: Millbrook Press, 2000.

Creasy, Edward S. *History of the Ottoman Turks: From the Beginnings of Their Empire to the Present Time.* London: Bentley, 1878.

Dijkstra, Henk, editor. *History of the Ancient & Medieval World,* Volume 11: *Empires of the Ancient World.* New York: Marshall Cavendish, 1996.

Kostich, Dragos D. *The Land and People of the Balkans: Albania, Bulgaria, Yugoslavia.* Philadelphia: Lippincott, 1973.

Sheehan, Sean. *Turkey.* New York: Marshall Cavendish, 1994.

Web Sites

"End of Europe's Middle Ages—Ottoman Turks." [Online] Available http://www.ucalgary.ca/HIST/tutor/endmiddle/ottoman.html (last accessed July 26, 2000).

"History 323: The Middle East in the Making: The History of the Ottoman Empire." [Online] Available http://www.humanities.ualberta.ca/ottoman/module2/lecture1.htm (last accessed July 26, 2000).

"Kosovo Field: As Bitter As Yesterday." [Online] Available http://www.megastories.com/kosovo/map/kosovof.htm (last accessed July 26, 2000).

The Ottoman Khilafa. [Online] Available http://www.naqshbandi.org/ottomans/ (last accessed July 26, 2000).

Pachacutec Inca Yupanqui

Died 1471

Inca emperor

Pachacutec Inca Yupanqui, sometimes referred to as Pacha-cuti, was not the first emperor of the Inca people in South America, but he was the first one whose existence is firmly established in history. More important, he was the greatest of the Inca rulers, an empire builder who began with a kingdom of perhaps twenty-five square miles and shaped it into a vast realm. He initiated a system of roads and a highly organized government that ruled its people efficiently and—by the standards of premodern America—with justice.

The achievements of Pachacutec were all the more remarkable in light of the fact that he was not his father's chosen successor, and that severe technological and administrative limitations faced the Incas. Not only did they lack the use of the wheel or of most pack animals, a handicap in their high mountain environment, but unlike the Aztecs or Maya, they did not even have a written language.

Roots of the Inca people

Though the term *Inca* is used to describe an entire na-

"Although his father and some other predecessors may have been at least partly legendary, Pachacuti was a real person, the actual founder of the Inca Empire and perhaps the greatest man produced in ancient America."

Jonathan Norton Leonard, Ancient America

tion, it was actually the name for its rulers. Thus the full name of their greatest emperor was Pachacutec Inca Yupanqui (pah-chah-KOO-tek ING-kuh yoo-PAHNG-kee). As for the Inca people, they emerged as a civilization in about 1100, when they established a capital named Cuzco (KOOZ-koh), or "navel of the world."

Perhaps because of the challenges imposed by the high Andes (AN-deez) Mountains where they lived in Peru, the Incas were not quick to begin building an empire. Only in the mid-1400s, during the reign of the semi-legendary Viracocha (veer-ah-KOH-kah)—whose name was taken from that of the Incas' principal deity, or god—did they begin to expand, and then only to an area about twenty-five miles around Cuzco.

Not the favorite son

Pachacutec was the son of Viracocha, but he was not his first or favorite son; still, his name meant "he who transforms the Earth," and he was destined to fulfill its promise. Due to the lack of written records, little is known about Pachacutec's life in general, much less his early life. Even the date of his birth is unknown.

At some point in the 1430s, the Incas were attacked by a neighboring tribe, and both Viracocha and his designated heir fled Cuzco for the safety of the mountains. Pachacutec, however, held his ground, and marshaled his army to drive back the invaders. With victory secured, he took the throne in 1438. That year is the beginning of Inca history, inasmuch as events after that point can be dated with relative certainty.

Building an empire

The Inca had no knowledge of other civilizations, even the Maya and Aztec, let alone those of Europe, Asia, and Africa. Nonetheless, Pachacutec's early career was much like that of **Genghis Khan** (see entry): first he rallied his supporters to deal with an outside threat, then he kept marching and built an empire.

Pachacutec set about strengthening his hold on the region around Cuzco, then his troops swept down the moun-

tains into a valley along the mighty Amazon River. They next marched northward along the highlands, conquering tribes as they went, before turning south to win the area around Lake Titicaca high in the Andes.

There was a purpose in Pachacutec's actions. He was not simply fighting battles; he was building a strong and unified empire. Wherever possible, he and his advisors won over neighboring tribes through diplomacy, or the art of negotiation. If other groups failed to listen to reason, however, they faced the wrath of the great Inca army, for which there was no equal in the region. Most tribes wisely agreed to bloodless conquest by the Incas.

Uniting the people

It was one thing to build an empire, and quite another to hold it together—something the descendants of Genghis

Inca warriors, from an ancient Peruvian painting. Pachacutec became the greatest Inca ruler by conquering his enemies and building a great empire. *Reproduced by permission of the New York Public Library Picture Collection.*

Jayavarman VII

The name Pachacutec is hardly a household word for most Westerners, even in America, though it deserves to be—and much the same can be said of Cambodia's Jayavarman VII (c. 1120–c. 1219). Just as Pachacutec built, but did not establish, the Inca Empire, so Jayavarman took the already established Khmer (k'MEER) or Angkor (AHNG-kohr) Empire to a much greater level than before. Not only was he—again like Pachacutec—an empire-builder in the sense that he conquered other lands, he too built in the literal sense. As Pachacutec rebuilt Cuzco after its destruction by enemies, Jayavarman built up two of the world's most extraordinary monuments, the temple cities of Angkor Wat and Angkor Thom (TOHM).

The Khmers, as the Cambodians of medieval times were known, had long been in contact with India, and had adopted the Hindu religion from the latter. The first powerful Khmer king, Jayavarman II (ruled c. 790–850), founder of the empire, established Hinduism as the state religion. Some time after 900, the Khmers carved Angkor Thom out of the jungle. Angkor Thom covered some five square miles, and included a moat, high walls, temples, palaces, and a tower, all carved in detail with images of Hindu gods.

Suryavarman II (ruled 1113–50) began the building of Angkor Wat, which is the more famous—though actually the smaller—of the two temple cities. He also conquered a number of surrounding kingdoms, but after his death the empire went into a period of decline when it was ruled first by the father and then the brother of Jayavarman VII.

Little is known about Jayavarman's early life, though it is clear he grew up as a member of the royal family in Angkor. His first wife was a devout Buddhist who strongly influenced him, but given the many similarities between Buddhism and

Khan, for instance, failed to do. Given their lack of a written language, it was all the more important for Pachacutec to impose a single spoken language on the people he conquered as a way of knitting them together. Soon the Incas' language, Quechua (KECH-oo-ah), became the region's lingua franca, a common language for people whose native languages differed.

To reduce threats from potentially hostile groups, Pachacutec sometimes ordered tribes to relocate. Thus he separated them from their homelands, where they might develop a base of support for future resistance. In line with his pol-

Hinduism—including its belief in reincarnation, or the cycle of repeated death and rebirth—this did not bring him into conflict with the established religion. After the death of his first wife, he married her sister, also a strong Buddhist.

Meanwhile, the empire weakened under his brother's rule, and the Champas in what is now Vietnam took the opportunity to invade. They even occupied Angkor Wat until Jayavarman VII drove them out in 1181. After achieving victory, he was crowned emperor at the age of sixty-one.

Jayavarman would live for thirty more years, during which time he expanded the empire into parts of what is now Vietnam, Laos, Malaysia, and Burma. Despite these conquests, however, he devoted most of his attention to extensive programs of building and rebuilding. Much of the glory of Angkor Thom and Angkor Wat are a result of his efforts to expand and beautify those cities; in addition, he built a large network of highways complete with rest houses, as well as some one hundred hospitals.

The pace of Jayavarman's building projects was extremely quick, and in some cases the workmanship shows this fact. It is likely that he felt a sense of urgency due to his advanced age. It is also possible that he suffered from leprosy, a dreaded disease involving gradual wasting of muscles, deformity, and paralysis, which was relatively common until modern times. Whatever the case, he lived to the age of ninety-one.

When he died, Jayavarman left behind considerable physical evidence that he had once ruled a great and mighty empire—an empire that, like the Incas', was doomed to be overtaken by outside invaders, in this case from Thailand. In 1431, about the time Pachacutec was beginning his career, the Thais completed their conquest of the Angkor Empire.

icy of not making Inca rule too harsh on the conquered peoples, however, Pachacutec's government pursued its relocation policy with care, for instance not moving people from the lowlands to the high mountains where the thin air and cold climate might cause deaths.

A highly organized state

Roads were another key element of Pachacutec's program to solidify his empire. Under his reign, the Incas constructed some 2,500 miles of stone roads, many of them across high mountain passes and others through steaming swamps. Though they were extremely well built, with tightly fitted stones, these were not roads as Europeans would understand them: most were only about three feet wide, which was sufficient to accommodate travelers on foot or load-bearing llamas (YAHM-uz). The latter, a relative of the camel, constituted the Incas' principal form of pack animal, though llamas could not carry anything like the weight supported by camels.

Along with the roads, the Incas built way stations placed at intervals equal to a day's travel, so that travelers could rest and obtain supplies. Trained runners traversed the road system, keeping the emperor abreast of events throughout his empire. Compared to the slow postal system of Europe (which, like that of the Inca Empire, was only for the use of the government, not ordinary citizens), the Incas' messenger service was extraordinarily fast and efficient. Thanks to the relay runners, who could transport a message at the rate of 140 miles a day, Pachacutec's army was never caught unawares by rebellions on their borders. In addition, the emperor kept troops stationed throughout the empire, ready to go into action whenever the alert was sounded.

It is hard to understand how the Incas managed to achieve their mighty feats of organization, given their lack of a written language. In order to run a government, it is necessary to keep records, particularly of inventory or supplies. In place of written records, the Incas under Pachacutec used an ingenious system of strings in varying lengths and colors, with which they recorded numerical information. For mathematical calculations, they made use of the abacus, an early form of calculator that used movable beads strung along parallel wires within a frame.

Turning over leadership to Topa

After years of administering his empire, Pachacutec turned over the reins of leadership to his son Topa. He continued to be actively involved in governmental affairs, however, particularly a program to rebuild Cuzco from the devastation of earlier attacks. He created a plan for the city and initiated vast building projects, including a huge central plaza surrounded by temples.

Topa, who ruled from 1471 to 1493, built on the gains made by his father, and his son Huayna Capac (WY-nuh KAH-pahk; ruled 1493–1525) controlled the empire at its height. By then the Incas held an area equal to that of the U.S. Eastern Seaboard, the coastal states from Maine to Florida. Under their rule were some 16 million people—an impressive number compared, for instance, to the population of England at the time, which was just 5 million.

The empire would not last long beyond Huayna Capac's time, and the arrival of Spanish explorers in 1533 signaled the beginning of a swift and merciless end to the Inca Empire. While it stood, however, it was one of the medieval world's most efficient, well-organized governments, and for this Pachacutec—whom many historians consider among the greatest rulers of all time—deserves much of the credit.

For More Information

Books

Baquedano, Elizabeth. *Aztec, Inca and Maya*. Photographs by Michel Zabé. New York: Knopf, 1993.

Brittan, Dolly. *The People of Cambodia*. New York: PowerKids Press, 1997.

Gonzalez, Maya Christina. *Inca Civilization*. Translated by Deborah Kent. Chicago: Children's Press, 1993.

Leonard, Jonathan Norton. *Ancient America*. Alexandria, VA: Time-Life Books, 1967.

Macdonald, Fiona. *Inca Town*. Illustrated by Mark Bergin, created and designed by David Salariya. New York: F. Watts, 1998.

Newman, Shirlee Petkin. *The Incas*. New York: F. Watts, 1992.

Web Sites

"Cambodia-Web: Origin of the Cambodians." *Cambodia-Web*. [Online] Available http://www.cambodia-web.net/history/history2.htm (last accessed July 26, 2000).

"Historical Summary of Cambodia." [Online] Available http://asia-tours.net/cambodia/history.html (last accessed July 26, 2000).

"Incas." [Online] Available http://www.travelvantage.com/per_inca.html (last accessed July 26, 2000).

St. Patrick

Born c. 396
Died c. 459

Roman-Irish saint

Patron saint of Ireland, St. Patrick remains one of the Middle Ages' most well-known saints, thanks in large part to the wild celebrations on his festival day on March 17. Wherever there are sons and daughters of Ireland—as in America, a country with far more people of Irish heritage than Ireland itself—there is plenty of merry-making on St. Patrick's Day.

Yet it might astound many to learn, first of all, that Patrick was not Irish; rather, he was a missionary, a religious teacher sent to people in a foreign land, from Roman-controlled Britain. Nor was he a particularly jolly figure, despite all the fun associated with his day. Furthermore, many of the feats attributed to him—for instance, driving all the snakes out of Ireland—are the product of medieval legend-making, not fact.

Sold into slavery

Patrick, or Patricius, was the son of Calpurnius, a minor Roman nobleman in Britain. Rome had controlled that island, whose people were of Celtic origin, for about four cen-

"Many tried to prevent this mission [to Ireland], and talked among themselves behind my back and said: 'Why is this fellow walking into danger among enemies who do not know God?'"

St. Patrick's Confessions

Portrait: *Reproduced by permission of Archive Photos, Inc.*

turies when Patrick was born. He lived at a time before the Roman Catholic Church had declared that its priests could not marry, and in fact his grandfather was a priest. Patrick's family were Christians, but as a boy he did not care much about religious matters, preferring to devote himself to pleasure. Then his life changed completely.

At the age of sixteen, Patrick was kidnapped by pirates, who carried him across the sea to the neighboring island of Ireland. There he was sold into slavery and forced to tend sheep. In his loneliness, he turned to prayer, and later wrote in his *Confessions:* "The love of God came to me more and more, and my faith was strengthened. My spirit was moved so that in a single day I would say as many as a hundred prayers, and almost as many in the night."

It was Patrick's belief that he had been enslaved as punishment from God. This was a common Christian idea, reflecting concepts from the Bible—for instance, the enslavement of the Israelites by the Babylonians, which the Hebrew prophets explained was a consequence of forsaking God. And just as he believed that God had caused his enslavement, Patrick at age twenty-two believed that God had called on him to escape from slavery.

Escape and return to Britain

In Patrick's *Confessions,* one of the few reliable sources about his life, he reported that one night he had a dream in which he was told to escape and return home. He crossed many miles to get to the Irish coast, he wrote, and there talked his way on to a ship bound for Britain. After three days of sailing, the ship landed, and the travelers journeyed for twenty-eight days through "wilderness" without finding any food.

Though the *Confessions* contains far fewer stories of miraculous occurrences than do later chronicles of Patrick's life, in some cases it is difficult to make sense of claims he made in the book. An example of this is the part about wandering for four weeks. Both Britain and France (Gaul at that time) are too small to contain a wilderness big enough—even in the early 400s—that people could be lost in it for a month.

In any case, Patrick was finally reunited with his family, and would probably have never left them had it not been for another dream. In this second vision, he said, he was told by a man to go to Ireland and convert the Irish to Christianity. It is possible Patrick's story of his life was influenced by passages from the Bible. The Old Testament tells how the children of Israel under Moses' leadership wandered for forty years in a tiny desert between modern-day Egypt and Israel, and the New Testament contains an account of the Apostle Paul being visited in a dream by a man from Greece who asked him to teach the Greeks about Christianity.

Priest and missionary

Feeling that he had heard from God, Patrick began preparing for the priesthood. He may have studied under Germain, a celebrated French saint, in the town of Auxerre (oh-SUR). He then asked church leaders to authorize his going to Ireland as a missionary, and at first they were skeptical—in part, he later wrote, because he was not very well educated, despite his noble birth.

Patrick finally gained permission to go to Ireland as the church's representative. Contrary to popular belief, he was not the first missionary sent to the Irish. A few years earlier, in 431, a missionary named Palladius had gone there, but his success had been limited.

Ireland at that time was dominated by pagan religions that worshiped many gods, most of them associated with natural forces. In fact the word *paganus* in Latin means "countryside-dweller," a reflection of the fact that at that time, Christianity's strongest influence was in large cities such as Rome. Ireland was mostly countryside, and Patrick was one of the first missionaries anywhere in the Christian world to preach mainly to country people.

Challenges in Ireland

Perhaps taking his cue from the Apostle Paul, who had lived about four centuries earlier, Patrick never spoke out actively against slavery, despite the fact that he had been a

A Gallery of Saints

The Middle Ages, as well as the late ancient period, produced literally thousands of figures who later became recognized as saints, Christians so devout that they served as a model to others. There were Roman Catholic saints such as **Bernard of Clairvaux** or **Joan of Arc,** and there were Eastern Orthodox saints such as **Cyril and Methodius;** then there were figures such as **Augustine** who were revered throughout the Christian world (see entries).

Some saints are particularly well known, primarily through popular legends that have little to do with the actual people themselves. Such is the case with St. Valentine, whose feast day on February 14 is even more well known than Patrick's on March 17. Perhaps these two events became so popular because they break up the dreariness of wintertime; in any case, the romantic associations of Valentine's Day have as little to do with the real St. Valentine as the feasting and drinking on St. Patrick's Day have to do with that saint.

There were at least three St. Valentines, one of whom lived in North Africa.

Of this one little is known, but slightly more information is available about the other two, one of whom was a priest in Rome, the other a bishop in another part of Italy (they may, in fact, have been a single person). Both—like their namesake in Africa—were martyred, or killed for their faith. The Roman priest seems to have died in 270, during persecutions under Emperor Claudius II. All three Valentines had feast days on February 14, when it was said that birds begin to pair off. There was also a pagan Roman custom associated with mid-February, whereby young men would draw the names of girls and pair up with them.

Then there is the saint associated with the most popular holiday of all: St. Nicholas, who as Santa Claus became a symbol of Christmas. In fact St. Nicholas was a bishop in Asia Minor (modern-day Turkey) during the late third century and early fourth century. The only possible link with Santa Claus is the fact that he was renowned for doing good deeds, and that he became a patron saint of children.

slave. He saw his mission as primarily a spiritual rather than a political one. Nonetheless, he expressed concern for the slaves who converted to Christianity, because he knew that they were far more vulnerable to persecution for their faith.

Many Irish leaders at that time were hostile to the new faith, and at one point Patrick and others with him were seized and imprisoned by a group of local kings. They were released two weeks later, but some time afterward, Patrick

St. George slaying a dragon. *Reproduced by permission of the Corbis Corporation.*

These characteristics led people in Western Europe to give gifts in his name at Christmastime, and eventually he was linked with a pagan figure from Scandinavia known as "Sint Klaes." During the nineteenth century, the Santa Claus legend began to take hold in America, where it bore almost no relation to the original St. Nicholas.

St. Nicholas also became one of the patron saints of Russia, along with St. Andrew. One version of the Russian flag used the cross of St. Andrew, a white X on a navy-blue field. This was also used by Scotland, which likewise claimed Andrew as a patron saint. Neighboring England's patron saint was George, and when these two countries were united as Great Britain in the early 1700s, the two saints' crosses helped form that nation's flag, the Union Jack.

The "real" St. George, like St. Nicholas, lived during the persecutions under Diocletian, the last Roman emperor before Constantine converted to Christianity in 312. It was said that George was a soldier beloved by Diocletian, but when he proudly announced the fact that he was a Christian, the emperor had him tortured and beheaded. Pictures of St. George typically show him in a classic medieval scene, as a knight slaying a dragon to rescue a lady. In Christian symbolism, however, this image has spiritual rather than romantic meaning: the dragon represents wickedness, and the lady stands for truth or the church.

managed to enrage the king of Tara. Patrick compared Tara, an Irish city, to Babylon, which was both the city where the Israelites were held captive for many years, and also a symbol of wickedness.

Tara had a pagan spring festival inaugurated each year by the king's lighting of a bonfire. However, one year the Christian holiday of Easter, commemorating Christ's death and resurrection, fell at the same time, and Patrick lit an Easter bonfire just before the king was supposed to light his. The king and his magicians, a later biographer wrote, went to attack Patrick, but the lead magician was suddenly pulled up into the air, then tossed to his death.

This miraculous and no doubt fictitious occurrence failed to stir the magicians, so Patrick engaged in a contest of miraculous powers with another magician. He triumphed, and the king of Tara made a half-hearted conversion to Christianity. The conversion became more sincere after the magician challenged one of Patrick's converts to another test, and failed miserably: according to this legend, both men were shut up in a house that was burned to the ground, and the Christian survived while the magician burned to death.

Patrick's writings

Whatever the truth of these stories, it appears certain that Patrick himself was subjected to a number of personal attacks. At some point in his youth, he confessed a past sin to a friend. It is not known what the sin was, but when the friend later had a falling-out with Patrick, he told a number of people about it, and this caused them to doubt Patrick's ability to lead Christians.

He wrote his *Confessions* in response to these accusations, and to claims that he had gotten rich as a minister of God. With regard to the latter complaints, Patrick admitted that wealthy people had tried to give him jewelry and other gifts, but he had refused them.

Patrick's other important writing was the *Epistle* (or letter), in which he responded to a British chieftain named Coroticus, who had killed some recent converts to Christianity, and sold others into slavery. The *Epistle* is a strong attack on Coroticus, who appears to have accepted Christianity earlier, though without much sincerity.

Mythology and fact

Little is known about how or when Patrick died, though it appears to have been in the mid-400s. In the period after his death, all sorts of amazing stories began to circulate about him. The story about Patrick driving all the snakes out of Ireland was probably invented as a way of explaining why Ireland has no native snakes—one of the few places in the world where this is true. Another legend associates him with the four-leaf clover, a symbol of Ireland, which he supposedly used as an illustration to explain to a pagan king about salvation in Christ.

Perhaps the most ironic aspect of the Patrick myth is the fact that Patrick, a figure revealed in his *Confessions* as an extremely serious, sober-minded, and humorless man whose concern was almost entirely for matters of the spirit, would be associated with a day known for feasting and drinking. But Patrick *did* convert the Irish, and the fact that Ireland remains one of the most staunchly Catholic countries on Earth is in part a tribute to him.

For More Information

Books

Bunson, Margaret and Matthew. *St. Patrick*. Huntington, IN: Our Sunday Visitor, 1993.

Dunlop, Eileen. *Tales of St. Patrick*. New York: Holiday House, 1996.

Reilly, Robert T. *Irish Saints*. Illustrated by Harry Barton. New York: Wings Books, 1992.

Tompert, Ann. *Saint Patrick*. Illustrated by Michael Garland. Honesdale, PA: Boyds Mills Press, 1998.

Web Sites

Catholic Online Saints and Angels. [Online] Available http://www.catholic.org/saints/index.shtml (last accessed July 26, 2000).

Patron Saints Index. [Online] Available http://www.catholic-forum.com/saints/indexsnt.htm (last accessed July 26, 2000).

Saints Lives. [Online] Available http://www.pitt.edu/~eflst4/saint_bios.html (last accessed July 26, 2000).

Marco Polo

Born 1254
Died 1324

Italian explorer

The journeys of Marco Polo were as remarkable in the Middle Ages as travel to another planet would be in modern times, and the information he brought back to Europe greatly expanded human knowledge. But his stories about faraway lands sounded so outrageous, and involved so many big numbers, that his neighbors nicknamed him "Marco Millions."

Setting out from his hometown of Venice, Italy, with his father and uncle in 1271, Marco was only seventeen years old when he began his travels. It would be twenty-four years before he returned to Europe, and during that time he would see half the known world. He would also have a series of amazing adventures, and would become personally acquainted with one of the medieval world's most remarkable rulers, **Kublai Khan** (see entry).

Venice and Cathay

In Marco Polo's time Venice was a powerful city-state, home to merchants and voyagers such as his father, Nicolo, and uncle, Maffeo. When Marco was six, Nicolo and Maffeo

"I have not told half of what I saw."

left Venice for Cathay (kah-THY), the name by which many Europeans knew China. At that time, China was under the control of the Mongols, nomadic warriors from Central Asia who conquered much of the world in the early 1200s.

Nicolo and Maffeo did not return for nine years, and during that time, Marco's mother died. When the two brothers came back to Venice in 1269, they came with a request from Kublai Khan (KOOB-luh; 1215–1294; ruled 1260–1294), the Mongol ruler of China, to the pope, head of the Catholic Church. The Great Khan, who respected all religions, wanted the pope to send a vial of holy oil, as well as a hundred religious teachers for his people. The Polos could not immediately obtain either, however, since the old pope had died and a new one had not yet been elected. An election could take months, and Nicolo and Maffeo were eager to begin their trip; therefore they set out for Cathay in 1271, taking seventeen-year-old Marco with them.

The adventure begins

They reached the city of Acre (AHK-ruh), an important church center in what is now Israel. There they met Tebaldo Visconti, a priest and representative of the Vatican— the pope's headquarters in Rome—who gave them letters for the Khan. From Acre they headed north to Cilicia (suh-LISH-uh), a region in southeastern Asia Minor, where they received word that a new pope had been elected: Tebaldo himself, who became Gregory X (ruled 1271–76). Therefore they returned to Acre, where Gregory blessed a vial of oil for the Khan.

As for teachers, however, Gregory could only spare two monks—and in the end, those two turned back when they realized how dangerous the trip to Cathay would be. But the Polos themselves were finally on their way, and they headed to Ormuz (ohr-MOOZ), a major seaport in Persia. The boats they saw there did not look particularly sturdy, however; therefore they decided to strike out for China over land.

A perilous journey

Today one can fly from Venice to Beijing, the Chinese capital—which under the reign of the Khans was called Khan-

balik (kahn-bah-LEEK)—in a few hours; Marco's journey, by contrast, took more than three years. He spent more than a year of that time in the mountains of Afghanistan, stricken with an unknown illness. Perhaps it was during this time that his father and uncle taught him the language of the Mongols, which they had mastered on their earlier trip. Marco also learned Farsi, or Persian, a common tongue for travelers and tradesmen in the East.

Finally, however, the Polos were able to resume their journey eastward, which took them across the Pamir (puh-MEER) range between Afghanistan and China. The Pamirs are among the world's highest mountains, and the journey—during which Marco saw an animal that came to be called the "Marco Polo sheep"—was a difficult one.

Coming down off the mountains, the travelers entered China itself, and for a long way, the going was relatively easy. Then they came to the Gobi Desert, which is nearly

Fourteenth-century painting of Marco Polo entering Beijing. *Reproduced by permission of the Granger Collection Ltd.*

the size of Alaska. It took the Polos thirty days of hard traveling to cross this extremely inhospitable region, even though
they did so at its narrowest part. At night, the desert winds
became so fierce they played tricks on the journeyers' minds,
and Marco later reported hearing voices calling to him in the
chilly darkness.

In the court of the Great Khan

Having crossed the Gobi, the Polos found themselves
in the heart of China. They followed the Yellow River, one of
that country's great waterways, until they met representatives
of the Great Khan who led them to Shang-tu (shahng-DOO).
The latter, known to Europeans by the name Xanadu (ZAN-
uh-doo), was the Khan's summer residence, some three hundred miles north of Beijing.

Though he must have seen China's Great Wall, Marco
never recorded the event. Yet there was much to impress him
when he and his father and uncle arrived at the court of the
Great Khan in May 1275. Kublai Khan, Marco later wrote, "is
the greatest Lord that is now in the world or ever has been."

Marco found the court at Shang-tu splendid, but not
as luxurious as the Khan's palace in Beijing. There, he reported, the Khan's four wives were attended by some forty thousand servants, and Marco himself dined at a banquet where
some six thousand guests were served all manner of delicacies.

As it turned out, Kublai was as impressed with Marco as
Marco was with him. While his father and uncle became involved in several successful business ventures, Marco spent
most of his time at court. During the corruption trial of an official, he testified regarding the man's dishonest actions, thus
showing his loyalty to the Khan. The latter therefore appointed
him to a series of offices which, over the next years, would vast-
ly extend the scope of Marco's already extraordinary travels.

Visions of the East

The Khan first sent Marco to the province of Yunnan
(yoo-NAHN), wedged between Tibet and Southeast Asia at
China's southwestern fringe. Marco thus became the first Eu-

ropean to see Tibet, one of the world's most remote and exotic lands. For three years beginning in 1282, he served as governor of Yangchow (yahng-ZHOH), a city along the Grand Canal of the Yangtze River (YAHNG-say) in east central China.

In the latter part of his governorship, Marco received orders to travel even farther: to India. On his way there, he visited a number of lands in southeast Asia: Champa, a kingdom in what is now central Vietnam; Thailand; Melaka, now part of Malaysia; and the island of Sumatra in modern Indonesia.

Crossing the enormous Bay of Bengal, Marco's boat touched land in the Andaman Islands, a part of India so remote that its people had never been exposed either to Hinduism or Buddhism, the country's two principal religions. The ship then sailed southward, to the island of Ceylon (seh-LAHN), the modern nation of Sri Lanka.

The way back

Marco probably arrived back in Beijing in 1287, when he was thirty-three years old. His aging father and uncle were ready to return home, but the Khan wanted them to stay; two years later, however, in 1289, Kublai allowed the three Europeans to accompany a Mongol princess to Persia, where she would marry the Mongol khan of that land. Various difficulties delayed their departure for some time, but finally in January 1292 the princess and the Polos, along with some six hundred passengers and crew on fourteen ships, set sail.

It was another long trip, taking nearly two years, during which time most of the passengers and crew died. Arriving in Ormuz, the Polos learned that Kublai was dead. It must have been with some sadness that they headed northward across land to the city of Trabzon (trab-ZAHN) on the Black Sea. From Trabzon they sailed to Constantinople, and on to Venice, and by the time they reached home in 1295, they had been gone nearly a quarter-century.

A teller of tall tales

But Marco's adventures were not over. Venice had gone to war with Genoa, another leading Italian city, and he

Ibn Battuta

His full name was Abu 'Abd Allah Muhammad ibn 'Abd Allah al-Lawati at-Tanji ibn Battuta; fortunately for non-Arabic speakers, however, he is known to history simply as Ibn Battuta (IB'n bah-TOO-tah; 1304–c. 1368). In spite of the fact that Marco Polo is much more well known outside the Arab world, in fact Ibn Battuta traveled much more widely. Over the space of twenty-nine years from 1325 to 1354, he covered some seventy-five thousand miles, three times the distance around Earth at the Equator—a particularly impressive feat at a time when the average person had seldom traveled more than a few miles from home.

Ibn Battuta was born into a wealthy family in the Moroccan city of Tangier (tan-JEER). He originally planned to study law, and when he went away on his first long journey at the age of twenty-one, he did so with the intention of later settling down. Like most people in Tangier, Ibn Battuta was a devout Muslim, or follower of the Islamic religion established by **Muham-** **mad** (see entry), and he planned to serve as an Islamic religious judge. His first trip, in fact, was a pilgrimage to the Muslim holy city of Mecca in what is now Saudi Arabia. This type of pilgrimage, called a *hajj* (HAHZH), is sacred to Islam, and all Muslims are encouraged to do it at least once. By the time of his death, Ibn Battuta had made the hajj a total of four times.

After his first hajj (1325–27), Ibn Battuta made a side trip into Persia. He returned to Mecca, thus completing a second hajj, then sailed along the east African coast to the trading city of Kilwa in the far south before returning to Mecca yet again in 1330. But he was just getting started: over the next three years, he journeyed through Turkey, the Byzantine Empire, and southern Russia, at that time part of the Mongol lands. He then passed through Afghanistan and other parts of Central Asia before entering India from the north.

Eventually Ibn Battuta wound up in the court of the ruthless sultan Muham-

became captain of a warship. In 1298, he was captured and thrown in a Genoese prison, where he met a writer named Rustichello (rus-ti-CHEL-oh).

Marco told Rustichello about his travels, and Rustichello began writing a book that would become known in English as *The Book of Ser Marco Polo the Venetian Concerning the Kingdoms and Marvels of the East,* or *The Description of the World.* The book would later be recognized as the basis for scientific geography, and greatly expanded Europeans' under-

Muslims gather to worship in the Great Mosque in Mecca. All Muslims are encouraged to make a pilgrimage to Mecca (a *hajj*) at least once; Ibn Battuta did it four times. *Reproduced by permission of the Library of Congress.*

mad ibn Tughluq (tug-LUK; ruled 1325–51; see box in Ala-ud-din Muhammad Khalji entry) in the great Indian city of Delhi (DEL-ee). Despite Tughluq's blood-

thirsty reputation, Ibn Battuta managed to remain in his service as a judge for eight years. Tughluq sent him on an official visit to the Mongol emperor of China, a later successor to Kublai Khan, but Ibn Battuta was shipwrecked, and never returned to Tughluq's court.

During the next few years, Ibn Battuta visited Ceylon, Southeast Asia, and China—possibly even as far north as the capital at Beijing. He then made the long journey home, stopping in Mecca a fourth time; but he quickly headed out again, this time to Muslim Spain and then south, across the Sahara into the splendid African empire of Mali.

Ibn Battuta stopped traveling in 1354, after which he sat down to write the record of his journeys in a volume translated as *The Travels of Ibn Battuta*. Along with all the other activity that filled his life, Ibn Battuta had many wives and children, and died when he was more than sixty years old.

standing of the world. Prior to Marco's mention of the Pamirs, for instance, no one in Europe had ever heard of those mountains. He was also the first European to describe places such as Tibet and Burma, lands that would not be visited again by people from the West until the 1800s.

Marco introduced Europeans to a wealth of new ideas, from paper money to playing cards. In addition, his book excited the interest of future explorers, among them Portugal's Prince **Henry the Navigator** (1394–1460; see entry), who virtually launched the Age of Exploration when he ordered a number of Portuguese voyages around the coast of Africa. The record of the Polos' difficult journey also affected a young sailor from Genoa named Christopher Columbus, who in 1492 set out to reach Cathay by sailing west—and instead discovered the New World.

Modern scholars believe Marco's reports to be amazingly accurate, though many of his neighbors had a hard time believing his tall tales. Later he married, had three daughters, and became a modestly successful merchant, but his reputation followed him to his death at age seventy. Relatives tried to get him to renounce what they thought were lies about deserts full of whispering voices and banquets with six thousand guests, but he refused; on his deathbed he announced, "I have not told half of what I saw."

For More Information

Books

Hull, Mary. *The Travels of Marco Polo*. San Diego, CA: Lucent Books, 1995.

MacDonald, Fiona. *Marco Polo: A Journey through China*. Illustrated by Mark Bergin, created and designed by David Salariya. New York: Franklin Watts, 1998.

MacDonald, Fiona. *The World in the Time of Marco Polo*. Parsippany, NJ: Dillon Press, 1997.

Roth, Susan L. *Marco Polo: His Notebook*. New York: Doubleday, 1990.

Twist, Clint. *Marco Polo: Overland to Medieval China*. Austin, TX: Raintree Steck-Vaughn, 1994.

Web Sites

Ibn Battuta's Trip. [Online] Available http://www.sfusd.k12.ca.us/schwww/sch618/islam/nbLinks/Ibn_Battuta_map_sites.html (last accessed July 26, 2000).

"Marco Polo and His Travels." *Silkroad Foundation*. [Online] Available http://www.silk-road.com/artl/marcopolo.shtml (last accessed July 26, 2000).

Marco Polo: His Travels and Their Effects on the World. [Online] Available http://www.geocities.com/TimesSquare/Maze/5099/sld001.html (last accessed July 26, 2000).

Other

Abercrombie, Thomas. "Ibn Battuta, Prince of Travelers." Photographs by James L. Stanfield. *National Geographic,* December 1991, pp. 2–49.

Rabia al-Adawiyya

Born c. 717
Died 801

Arab mystic

A mystic is someone who seeks direct contact with God through meditation or special insight. Mystics believe this is possible—indeed, *only* possible—outside the context of formal religion. But this unorthodox approach does not mean that mystics expect a "shortcut," as the life and teachings of an extraordinary woman named Rabia al-Adawiyya illustrate.

Founder of the Sufis, a sect of Islamic mystics, Rabia was sold into slavery; she gained her freedom, according to some legends, because her master was awed by a miraculous light shining above her head. She devoted her life to a quest for direct contact with Allah, or God.

"O God, if I worship Thee in fear of Hell, burn me in Hell; and if I worship Thee in hope of Paradise, exclude me from Paradise; but if I worship Thee for Thine own sake, withhold not Thine everlasting beauty."

Prayer attributed to Rabia

Sufi mysticism

The Middle Ages was a time when mysticism proliferated in lands influenced by the great religions of the Middle East: Judaism, Christianity, and Islam. Some of these mystics would be judged insane if they lived in modern times; others were fanatics of one kind or another who used mysticism as a mask for darker urges within themselves. Then there were the genuine seekers, among them Rabia al-Adawiyya (rah-BEE-ah al-ah-dah-WEE-ah).

Rabia is generally credited as the founder of the Sufis, whose name comes from a word meaning "wool." They reacted to the political turmoil of their times, an age when the Abbasid caliphate was extending its power throughout the Muslim world, by retreating to an inner search for God. A principal belief of the Sufis was that one should not worship Allah out of fear of Hell, or hope of Heaven; rather, love for God should be an end in itself.

The daughter of Ismail

The details of Rabia's life are sketchy, though it appears she was born in about 717. Her mother and her father, Ismail (EES-my-el), a holy man committed to a life of poverty, lived on the edge of the desert near the town of Basra in what is now Iraq. They had four daughters, each of whom they named Rabia, with an additional name to distinguish them; the famous Rabia was the fourth.

The "facts" of Rabia's biography are generally no more than legends, an example of which is a story surrounding her birth. Due to their poverty, the parents had no oil in their house on the night she was born, which meant that they could not anoint (pour oil on) the navel of their newborn child, as was the custom. Ismail refused to beg from his neighbors, and this caused his wife to weep. Upset, the father knelt in the darkness and fell asleep, whereupon he had a dream in which the prophet **Muhammad** (see entry) told him: "Do not be sad. The girl child who has just been born is a queen amongst women." He was told that his faith would be rewarded, and soon afterward, the governor of the region gave him money for the raising of his daughter.

Sold into slavery

When Rabia was about eleven years old, Ismail died, and the mother, hoping to find a better life for her children, took them to Basra. On the way, however, bandits attacked

them, killing the mother and kidnapping the girls. Rabia, along with her sisters, was sold into slavery.

Eventually she wound up in Baghdad, a great city of the Islamic world that is today the capital of Iraq. There a man bought her, and proceeded to exploit her talents. Not only was she beautiful—she would receive many proposals of marriage in her life, each of which she refused—but she was a talented singer. Therefore he put her to work entertaining people, and he lived well off the money she earned.

The song changes

It was said that during this time, Rabia became affected by the world around her, and adopted loose ways. Then one day when she was about thirty-six, she was singing before a wedding party when suddenly, the song inside of her

The Whirling Dervishes represent a branch of the Sufis, Islamic mystics whose founder was Rabia al-Adawiyya. *Reproduced by permission of the Corbis Corporation.*

changed. Instead of singing to the wedding guests, she found herself singing to Allah.

From then on, she refused to sing for anyone but God, and this angered her master. He began to abuse her, but still she refused to resume her old life. At this point the legends about Rabia differ. Some say that her master was overwhelmed by a light shining above her head, which illuminated his whole house, and therefore he freed her. Others maintain that he grew so frustrated with her that he sold her at a market, where a holy man bought her.

Only one love

Whatever the case, it was said that the holy man took her to his home and treated her with kindness. He did not expect her to be his slave, he explained, but if she would be his wife, he would marry her. She thanked him, but said that she had no desire to marry anyone.

Legends maintain that Rabia soon came in contact with Hasan al-Basri (bahs-REE; 642–728), a noted Islamic leader. This is difficult to accommodate with the few known facts about her, since when Hasan died she would have only been thirty-seven, and tales of their conversations suggest that they knew each other for a long time. Regardless of the details, the distinguished Hasan came into her life, and like the holy man before him, asked her to marry him. Again she refused him, explaining that her only love was Allah.

A woman in a world of men

Another story about Rabia and Hasan is that one day when she was sitting by a lake, he spread his prayer mat on the surface of the water, where it floated miraculously. She had a prayer mat too, as did all Muslims, for the purpose of praying toward the holy city of Mecca five times a day, and she caused her mat to rise into the air with her on it. Then she told Hasan that "the real business is outside these tricks. One must apply oneself to the real business."

The "real business" was a quest for the direct knowledge of God, and it is a testament to Rabia's reputation that

Julian of Norwich

In the Islamic world of the Middle Ages, it was highly unusual that a woman would become an influential religious leader, as Rabia al-Adawiyya did. It was hardly less remarkable, in that day and age, that a woman in England would become respected as a mystic visionary; but that was the case with Julian of Norwich (1342–c. 1420), author of the first writings in English by a woman.

Julian is a man's name; as for the real name of "Julian of Norwich," which came from the fact that she lived in a cell attached to the Church of St. Julian in Norwich, England, it will probably never be known. She was an anchorite, a term for a type of nun or monk who lives completely alone.

It was said that when she was about thirty, Julian very nearly died, and indeed a priest was prepared to administer the last rites to her. On her deathbed, she looked up at a crucifix, a cross bearing a representation of the dying Jesus, and suddenly the cross began to glow. Julian was revived, and lived another four decades.

During that time, she underwent a great deal of physical hardship, as befit her chosen life of self-denial. She wrote down her revelations, or "showings," which were much more optimistic than those of most medieval mystics. Typically mystics tended to write about hellfire and judgment, but Julian's most famous statement was "All shall be well." In the twentieth century, the highly acclaimed poet T. S. Eliot adapted this line in one of his poems.

legends of her—whether or not they were true—depict her as giving religious teaching to the esteemed Hasan. Women were second-class citizens in most parts of the medieval world, and this was certainly true in Islam. Thus it was later said of Rabia, "When a woman walks in the ways of Allah like a man she cannot be called a woman." Other admirers compared her to the Virgin Mary, mother of Christ.

Rabia's teachings

Rabia was speaking of both men and women when she said that there were three kinds of men: one who uses his hands to gain wealth in this world, one who uses his hands to pray for rewards in the afterlife, and one who allows his hands to be tied by God—to serve without expecting anything in return.

This was the essence of the Sufi teaching, which she expressed in a famous prayer quoted in a variety of forms. One version was: "O God, if I worship You for fear of Hell, burn me in Hell, and if I worship You in hope of Paradise, exclude me from Paradise. But if I worship You for Your own sake, grudge me not Your everlasting beauty." Another time, she explained that both fire, or Hell, and the Garden, or Heaven, were "veils" that kept the seeker from a true knowledge of God.

A life of self-denial

In line with her belief that the seeker should not expect anything in return, Rabia, like many other mystics, lived a life of self-denial. She would often fast, or go without food, for long periods of time, and she lived in poverty. She welcomed misfortune, she said, because it was no better than blessings: all things were from Allah, and therefore they were good.

One legend told that while making the pilgrimage to Mecca, an act to which Muslims were called, her donkey died in the middle of the desert. The people on the caravan she was with offered to help her, but she refused, saying she would stay in the desert and trust in Allah. It was said that after she nearly died, she prayed to God, and he restored the donkey's life.

A woman of faith

Whatever the truth of the many legends ascribed to her, there is no doubt that Rabia was a woman of powerful faith, and that her influence spread far beyond her lifetime. The Sufis remained an influential sect throughout the Middle Ages, and continue to flourish today.

From the few remaining details of her life, it appears that Rabia left Baghdad at some point and settled in Basra again. She lived there for many years, then journeyed to Jerusalem, another holy city in the Muslim world. She died and was buried there.

Joachim of Fiore

Few medieval mystics influenced modern thinking as much as Joachim of Fiore (y'wah-KEEM, FYOHR-ay; c. 1130–c. 1202), an Italian monk of the Cistercian (sis-TUR-shun) order. In 1185, he began writing a commentary on the biblical book of Revelation, which describes the end of the world. To do his writing, he had separated himself even from other monks, but he soon attracted followers, and in 1196 they were recognized as a Cistercian order known as the Florensians.

Late in life, Joachim began to believe that he had been given special insights on history, and began writing these down just before his death in 1202. Though his ideas were radical, and would lead to a number of interpretations that later troubled church leaders, they received the approval of Pope Innocent III.

Joachim's ideas were based on the Christian concept of the Trinity: God the Father, God the Son, and God the Holy Spirit. Later followers interpreted his view of history to suggest that there were three ages, each consisting of forty-two generations. They were living, they believed, in the Age of the Son, and in about 1260, the world would enter the Age of the Spirit, when love and freedom would reign.

No serious student of the Middle Ages would accept the idea that love and freedom became universal at any point during that era, or at any time since. However, the idea of three ages seeped into the popular consciousness, and is the source of the prevailing notion of three historical ages: ancient, medieval, and modern.

For More Information

Books

Arvey, Michael. *The End of the World: Opposing Viewpoints.* San Diego, CA: Greenhaven Press, 1992.

Muhaiyaddeen, M. R. Bawa. *Sufi Stories for Young Children.* Philadelphia, PA: Fellowship Press, 1992.

Stewart, Desmond. *Early Islam.* New York: Time-Life Books, 1967.

Web Sites

Denlinger, Gretchen. "Julian of Norwich's Revelations." [Online] Available http://www.millersv.edu/~english/homepage/duncan/med-fem/julian1.html (last accessed July 26, 2000).

"Joachimites." [Online] Available http://topaz.kenyon.edu/projects/margin/joachim.htm (last accessed July 26, 2000).

"Julian of Norwich (1342–ca. 1416)." [Online] Available http://www.luminarium.org/medlit/julian.htm (last accessed July 26, 2000).

"Julian of Norwich Shrine." [Online] Available http://home.clara.net/clara.net/f/r/m/frmartinsmith/webspace/julian/ (last accessed July 26, 2000).

Sufism/Islamic Mysticism. [Online] Available http://www.digiserve.com/mystic/Muslim/F_start.html (last accessed July 26, 2000).

Richard I

Born 1157
Died 1199

English king

Richard I, better known as Richard the Lionheart or Richard the Lion-Hearted, was one of the Middle Ages' most celebrated and romantic figures. He was immortalized in the tales of Robin Hood and in countless legends, and centuries later in the novel *Ivanhoe* by Sir Walter Scott. Yet when one studies his actual career and character, it is hard to understand why.

Richard deserves a place among England's worst kings, though perhaps he cannot be judged in those terms since he spent all but six months of his ten-year reign away from England. In fact he cared much for France, his homeland, and for his wars in faraway places, most notably the Third Crusade (1189–92). Despite the fact that he was a sometimes talented military leader—one of his few actual merits—the crusade was a disaster, and for Richard it ended with his being kidnapped by a noble he had insulted. He allowed the English people to pay his ransom, a sum that has been estimated as the equivalent of $100 billion in today's dollars.

> "I am born of a rank which recognizes no superior but God."

Statement by Richard to Emperor Henry VI, while awaiting his ransom by the English people

Portrait: *Reproduced by permission of the Corbis Corporation.*

Family feud

Richard was the son of Henry II and **Eleanor of Aquitaine** (see entry), both of whom were French by birth, and throughout his lifetime he remained more emotionally attached to France than to England. Not only did he hold the title "duke of Aquitaine" (Aquitaine was a region in France), but his first language was French, and some historians maintain that he despised his adopted country, England—the country he hoped one day to rule.

Richard was one of four brothers, all of whom fought constantly with one another; thus when his younger brother John (see box in Eleanor of Aquitaine entry) later seized the throne in Richard's absence, he was only carrying on a family tradition. Richard's fortunes were helped by the death of his two older brothers, Henry and Geoffrey, and this left him with only one other significant male rival: his father.

In his early twenties, Richard allied himself with a contemporary, Philip II Augustus of France (ruled 1179–1223) against Henry. By the time he was thirty-two, in 1189, Richard had his father on the run, and chased him across France. Forcing his father to surrender, he demanded that the latter declare him his rightful heir, and when Henry died a few weeks later, Richard mourned little. (It should be noted that Henry was no saint: in 1170, he had ordered the murder of **Thomas à Becket**, Archbishop of Canterbury [see English Scholars, Thinkers, and Writers entry], and had treated Eleanor so badly that she became his sworn enemy.)

Setting off for the crusade

More than ninety years before, armies from Western Europe had subdued parts of the Holy Land in the Middle East, declaring that the birthplace of Christ had finally been placed under Christian rule. In fact Jesus, with his message of love and compassion, would hardly have recognized his alleged followers' "Christian" behavior, which included looting and murder. In the years since, European gains in the Holy Land had slowly melted in the face of a growing Muslim resistance, and in Richard's time the Saracens (as Europeans scornfully called Muslims) had an especially formidable leader in **Saladin** (see entry). The latter had scored a particularly humiliating victory against the crusaders in 1188, and this sparked the Third Crusade.

From the moment he heard about the crusade, Richard wanted to take part; but as with many another crusader, he was motivated more by worldly aims than by spiritual ones. Richard was a gifted if sometimes reckless warrior, and he longed for the glory of battle. Therefore he began setting his affairs in order, preparing to leave. He placed John in charge during his absence, and began raising money wherever he could find it. Richard's upkeep would prove costly for the English people, particularly the country's sole ethnic minority, the Jews. The latter were taxed heavily by Richard, and it was an ill omen for his reign that his coronation on September 3, 1189 sparked a wave of anti-Semitic riots that lasted for half a year.

Finally Richard was prepared to leave for the crusade, in which he would be joined by Philip and the Holy Roman Emperor **Frederick I Barbarossa** (see Holy Roman Emperors entry). The latter drowned on his way to the Holy Land, however, and Duke Leopold of Austria—a man who was destined to figure heavily in Richard's future—took his place.

The journey to Acre

Philip arrived in Palestine ahead of Richard, who had taken a couple of detours on his way. Traveling by sea, he stopped in Sicily to visit the king there, an unwise move that angered Barbarossa's successor, Henry VI, a foe of Sicily; and he also managed to get married. His bride was Berengaria (bayr-un-GAR-ee-uh), daughter of the king of Navarre (nuh-VAHR) in Spain, and this too was an unwise political move. Richard had promised Philip that he would marry a French princess, and Philip rightly saw that intended marriage— kings in the Middle Ages usually married for power, not love—as a means of strengthening his power base.

Richard also took time to fight a war on the island of Cyprus, but finally he arrived in Palestine—just in time to catch a case of malaria that rendered him too sick for battle. Philip was in the middle of a siege, or a sustained assault, on the city of Acre (AHK-ruh), and Richard had to be carried to the siege on a litter, a decorated contraption resembling a stretcher.

By mid-1191, Richard had recovered from his illness sufficiently to lead the troops, and he was rightly given much of the credit when the city fell to the crusaders on July 12. But now it was Philip's turn to get sick, or at least that was what he claimed. He made a hasty retreat to France, where he spread rumors that Richard was living a life of ease in the Holy Land. Worse, he began plotting with John to help the latter take the English throne.

Richard and Saladin

Richard, meanwhile, created more troubles for himself when he insulted Leopold of Austria. In his view, the latter was a mere duke, and not qualified to place his standard, or royal flag, alongside that of a king; therefore Richard ordered that Leopold's standard be flung down into the mud. He would later regret his haughty action, but in the meantime he faced another formidable enemy: Saladin.

Many legends would later circulate concerning these two great leaders, though in fact they never actually met. They fought several battles, and at the city of Arsuf Richard scored a brilliant victory against Saladin's much larger force. He also displayed his ruthlessness in killing Muslim prisoners, reasoning that since they were "infidels" or ungodly people in his view, the same rules did not apply to them as to Christians.

Richard's war in Palestine was as much a matter of negotiation as it was of battle. His dealings were with Saladin's brother Saphadin (sah-fah-DEEN), to whom he took a liking. At one point he even suggested that his sister Joan marry Saphadin, a highly unorthodox move since she was a Christian and he a Muslim. But neither was willing to convert, so the idea was dropped.

A hasty retreat

Like many another crusader, Richard hoped to attack the holy city of Jerusalem, but as he prepared for his assault, he met with a number of problems. His most trusted lieutenant, Conrad of Montferrat (mawn-fay-RAHt), was killed by the Assassins, a fanatical sect of Islamic terrorists. Then an

Errol Flynn as Robin Hood in the 1938 film *The Adventures of Robin Hood*. The Robin Hood tales painted a picture of Richard I as noble and valiant—quite different from reality. *Reproduced by permission of the Kobal Collection.*

epidemic spread among his men, who were not accustomed to the climate in Palestine; and finally, he learned about Philip and John's plot against him. He gave up his plans for the attack, and began preparing to return home.

The Third Crusade had ended in disaster, and Richard, who had managed to make even more enemies among his allies than among the Muslims, needed to make a hasty retreat. He paid a group of pirates from Romania to smuggle him out, but on the way they were shipwrecked on the Adriatic Sea, which lies between Italy and the Balkan Peninsula. In Vienna, Austria, he became aware that his old foe Duke Leopold was in pursuit, but by then it was too late: Leopold's soldiers had captured him.

Kidnap and ransom

Leopold turned Richard over to Henry VI, the emperor, who had him imprisoned. His kidnappers sent word to England demanding a ransom of 100,000 marks (the German currency) and 200 hostages. If the estimate of $100 billion is to be believed, this would be the equivalent of a foreign power kidnapping the U.S. president and demanding to receive more than half of all the income tax paid by corporations to the federal government, or more than a third of the total defense budget, in the late twentieth century—an almost inconceivable sum.

Richard, however, seems to have never been in doubt that his subjects would pay the ransom, which of course meant raising their already high taxes. "I am born of a rank which recognizes no superior but God," he told the emperor. Meanwhile John tried to seize the throne, but Eleanor prevented him; and Richard, who had made friends with the emperor, ensured that Henry would give no aid to John. Henry was so taken with Richard, in fact, that after receiving the first installment of the ransom money, he released him.

An expensive ruler

One reason for his early release was the fact that Henry knew Richard would make war on the French, enemies of the Holy Roman Empire—and this is in fact what Richard spent the six remaining years of his life doing. He built a huge network of castles across England and France, and when he had trouble raising a fighting force among the knights of England, he employed mercenaries (soldiers who will fight for whoever pays them) to help him.

All of these measures proved extraordinarily costly, and placed additional burdens on his people. Normally the

English king received 30,000 pounds (the English unit of money) in a year—but Richard spent 49,000 pounds one year just on building castles. Richard placed ever-increasing demands for money on England, and these only stopped when he died from a battle wound that developed gangrene.

The legend and the reality

Handsome and dashing, Richard was in some ways ideally suited to become a figure of legend, as he did. But his character could not be more different from that of the noble, valiant knight that the legends made him. It was particularly ironic that he was linked with Robin Hood, the fictional robber who took from the rich and gave to the poor.

Actually, Robin Hood may not have been so fictional: a headstone on the grave of Robert, Earl of Huntington (died 1247), proclaims that he was the "real" Robin Hood. But this Robin Hood was as different from his legend as Richard was from his: Robert stole from both the rich and the poor, and gave to himself.

For More Information

Books

Jessop, Joanne. *Richard the Lionhearted.* Illustrated by Martin Salisbury. New York: Bookwright Press, 1989.

Storr, Catherine. *Richard the Lion-Hearted.* Illustrated by Peter Gregory. Milwaukee, WI: Raintree Children's Books, 1987.

Suskind, Richard. *The Crusader King: Richard the Lionhearted.* Illustrated by William Sauts Bock. Boston: G. K. Hall, 1973.

Welch, Ronald. *Knight Crusader.* New York: Oxford University Press, 1979.

Web Sites

Löwenherz, Richard. "Richard Lionheart." [Online] Available http://www.ping.at/kessler/index1.html (last accessed July 26, 2000).

"Richard the Lion Heart." [Online] Available http://intranet.ca/~magicworks/knights/richard.html (last accessed July 26, 2000).

Saladin

Born 1138
Died 1193

Kurdish-Egyptian sultan and warrior

Assessing the career of Saladin more than eight centuries after his death, French historian René Grousset echoed a sentiment often expressed in Saladin's own lifetime. In Grousset's opinion, the Muslim leader's devotion to God—without the extremism that sometimes goes with such faith—expressed the virtues of generosity and kindness prized by the Europeans who fought against him in the Third Crusade (1189–92).

Thus Saladin won as many admirers among the "Franks," as the Muslims disdainfully called the European invaders, as he did from people on his own side. Indeed, Saladin came much closer to the ideals of knighthood than most crusaders—including **Richard I** (see entry), with whom he was often associated in later legends.

Arabs, Turks, and Kurds

The center of the Islamic world was and is the Arab lands of the Middle East. Yet when the Western Europeans launched the Crusades (1095–1291), an effort to take control

"It is equally true that his generosity, his piety, devoid of fanaticism, that flower of liberality and courtesy which had been the model of our old chroniclers, won him no less popularity in Frankish Syria than in the lands of Islam."

René Grousset

Portrait: *Reproduced by permission of the Corbis Corporation.*

of Palestine from the Muslims, leadership over the region had passed from the Arabs to the Seljuk Turks. By the time of Saladin (SAL-uh-din), however, there was a power vacuum in the Muslim world, and this in part made his rise possible.

Born Salah ud-Din Yusuf ibn Ayyub, Saladin—the latter is the name by which the crusaders knew him—was neither an Arab nor a Turk, but a Kurd. Ethnically related to Iranians, the Kurds had no national government of their own, but inhabited a region in the area where the borders of modern-day Turkey, Iran, Iraq, and Syria join. Saladin himself was born in what is now Iraq, but spent much of his youth in Damascus, Syria.

Meets Nur ad-Din

Damascus was one of the principal culture centers of the Muslim world, and it was there that Saladin's father, Ayyub, served as an official. As a youth, Saladin took advantage of the educational opportunities in the great city, and at one point seemed destined to become a scholar of religion and the law. But he was brought up to be a warrior and a leader, and ultimately events would point him in that direction.

At the age of fourteen, Saladin traveled to Aleppo, a major Syrian city, to live with his uncle, Shirkuh (sheer-KOO). Shirkuh held a senior command under Nur ad-Din (noor ed-DEEN; 1118–1174), sultan or king of Syria, who had played a decisive role in defeating the Europeans in the Second Crusade (1147–49). By the age of eighteen, Saladin was working under Shirkuh, but he soon attracted the notice of Nur ad-Din, who took the young man into his trusted inner circle.

Founds Ayyubid dynasty

From 1164 to 1169, when Saladin was in his mid- to late twenties, Egypt was in a state of civil war. The country had long been ruled by a group called the Fatimids (FAT-uh-midz), but as their dynasty had declined, Muslim leaders such as Nur ad-Din sought to extend their control to Egypt. Saladin accompanied the sultan on the Egyptian campaign, gaining valuable experience there.

In 1171, Saladin led Nur ad-Din's forces to victory in Egypt, abolishing the Fatimids and establishing his own Ayyubid (uh-YÜ-bid) dynasty, named after his father. This put him at odds with Nur ad-Din, and the two might have had a serious clash, but in 1174 Saladin's whole world changed. That year marked the death of three men: Nur ad-Din, Shirkuh, and Amalric (uh-MAL-rik; ruled 1163–74), the king of European-controlled Jerusalem.

Facing Muslim foes

In his latter days, Shirkuh had served as vizier (viz-EER), or administrator, of Syria, and Saladin now took over this important post. This put him in a very powerful position: by conquering the Fatimids, he controlled not only Egypt— one of the key centers of the Islamic world—but Libya and the western and southern portions of the Arabian Peninsula.

His role in Syria was a more touchy matter, since the country remained under the official control of the caliph, or leader of the Arab Muslims, in Iraq. The once-powerful Abbasid (uh-BAHS-id) caliphate, however, was past its prime, and the caliph rightly regarded Saladin as a threat. Because he lacked real control over his declining empire, however, the caliph was forced to recognize Saladin's power in the region.

The caliph was not Saladin's only foe on the Muslim side. A mysterious group had been formed in Iran in 1090, and their name would eventually enter the languages of Europe as a term for a type of terrorist who kills political leaders: the Assassins. Due to disagreements with Saladin's interpretation of the Islamic faith, the Assassins tried on two occasions, in 1174 and 1175, to take his life.

Saladin survived the attacks, however, and went on to further establish his role as leader by marrying Nur ad-Din's widow, Ismat (ees-MAHT). She remained his favorite wife. Returning to Egypt, he enjoyed a short period of peace, in which the Egyptian economy flourished, and he established several Muslim colleges. By 1177, however, he was on the warpath, beginning a series of engagements that would occupy most of his remaining years.

Leaders of the First Crusade

Saladin was undoubtedly one of the most colorful figures of the Crusades, but many of the most significant European leaders were the knights who fought in the First Crusade (1095–99) forty years before his birth. Among these were the Normans Bohemond I (BOH-ay-maw; c. 1050–1111) and his nephew Tancred (c. 1078–1112).

Son of Robert Guiscard (gee-SKARD), who with his brother Roger controlled much of Italy in the eleventh century, Bohemond had first distinguished himself by helping his father take Rome from Emperor **Henry IV** (see dual entry on Gregory VII and Henry IV) in 1094. Much of what is known about him comes from **Anna Comnena** (see Historians entry), and it is not a pretty sight: in Anna's estimation, Bohemond was greedy and uncouth, interested in nothing but his own advancement. In 1098 he led the crusaders in the capture of Antioch in Syria, and went on to become its ruler, but in the following year he was captured by the Turks while trying to take another city. Released in 1103, he spent his latter years in an unsuccessful campaign against the Byzantines.

After fighting alongside his uncle at Antioch and other cities, Tancred became leader of a succession of cities in the Holy Land. Like many of the victorious crusaders, he amassed a fortune, and also spent his latter days fighting against his fellow Christians, the Byzantines. Historians of the medieval era often portrayed him as a gallant knight, but the facts do not match this idealized image: Tancred's July 1099 assault on Jerusalem was almost unbelievably brutal. He and his troops slaughtered thousands of Muslims, even going so far as to break into mosques and murder the worshipers there.

Another romanticized figure was Godfrey of Bouillon (boo-YAWn; c. 1060–1100), a French nobleman. In 1099, he gained the title "protector of the Holy Sepulchre" (SEP-ul-kur, the place where Christ had supposedly been laid to rest after his crucifixion), and defended the crusaders' gains against an invading force

First moves against the crusaders

A Turkish victory over the Byzantine Empire in 1176 removed a powerful potential adversary from the field, and Saladin resolved that it was time to remove the crusaders—who controlled most of the coastal areas of what is now Israel and Lebanon—for good. After a series of victories, he agreed to a truce with the crusaders in 1179.

Godfrey of Bouillon has been idealized as the perfect Christian knight. *Reproduced by permission of Archive Photos, Inc.*

Godfrey's brother Baldwin (c. 1058–1118) was certainly not an example of high character. In 1098, he established the first crusader state by double-crossing a fellow Christian, the Armenian prince Thoros, and taking control of his lands. After the death of Godfrey, he set about establishing control over as much of the Holy Land as possible, and this put him into conflict with another Christian, his fellow crusader Tancred. Having earlier married an Armenian princess to secure his control over Thoros's realm, he later left her for a Sicilian countess; but since he had not gotten a divorce from the first wife, his second marriage was annulled, or declared illegal. He died on a raiding expedition into Egypt.

By contrast to most of the knights of the First Crusade, Raymond IV (1042–1105), count of Toulouse (tuh-LOOS) in France, won the admiration of the Byzantines. Anna Comnena wrote that her father, the emperor, even treated Raymond like a son. Raymond also fought against Bohemond, and founded the crusader state of Tripoli in Lebanon.

from Egypt. It is possible that legends about him—particularly his portrayal as a sincere believer in the stated purpose of the Crusades as a "holy war"—were accurate. In any case, the fact that he was handsome and dashing and died young helped spawn stories about Godfrey as a perfect Christian knight.

No doubt he was hoping to buy time for an even more forceful attack; in 1183, however, Muslim forces in several key Syrian cities revolted against him, and this diverted Saladin's attention for some time. Also, in 1185 he contracted a disease (the nature of the illness is not known) that would continue to weaken him for the rest of his life. Yet in 1187, he scored one of the greatest victories of his career.

Victory at Hittin

The site of the battle was Hittin or Hattin, and the leader of the opposing force was a flamboyant knight named Reynaud de Chatillon (ray-NOH duh SHAH-tee-yawn) who had been attacking Saladin's supply caravans. Reynaud was even threatening the Muslim holy city of Mecca, and Saladin's response was to bring an army of more than twenty-five thousand men to Hittin.

Recognizing that in the dry countryside of the Middle East, control of the water supply was the key to victory, Saladin cut the crusaders off from all sources of water. The parched European force camped on the night of July 3, 1187, and all night long Saladin's troops beat war drums and chanted to frighten their enemies.

At dawn, the crusaders found themselves facing the Muslims in the east, and thus the light of the Sun made it hard to see them; furthermore, its rays beating down on their chain-mail armor only added to the Europeans' heat exhaustion. Saladin dealt the crusaders a devastating defeat, killing many—including Reynaud, who was executed—and capturing many others, who were then sold into slavery.

The Second Crusade begins

Despite his harsh treatment of the Christians at Hittin, Saladin was generally far more humane in his treatment of the enemy than the crusaders themselves were. Stories of his kindness abounded: for instance, when his troops captured a Christian baby, he saw to it that the infant was returned to its mother. He had even been kind to one of the crusaders' leaders, King Guy (GEE) of Jerusalem, who he had allowed to go free after capturing him in battle.

Saladin would live to regret this last decision, when Guy launched a siege, or attack, on a Muslim fortress at Acre (AHK-ruh) in what is now Israel. This would in turn spark the Second Crusade, which brought a whole new set of armies into battle under the command of Richard I and King Philip of France.

The greatest setback of Saladin's career was the surrender of Acre after a two-year siege in July 1191. Richard massacred the city's defenders in retaliation for Hittin, then set his eyes on Jerusalem. The result was a fifteen-month conflict between the two leaders, both legendary figures whose battles would inspire many famous tales.

Fighting Richard

Though Richard never made it to Jerusalem, he gave Saladin fierce competition. Saladin defeated the Christian forces near Arsuf (ar-SOOF) on September 7, 1191, but in the skirmishes that followed, he discovered that few Muslim forces were willing to face the formidable Richard in battle. In the end, he kept Richard away from Jerusalem using the same strategy that had won him victory at Hittin: control of the water supply.

The last battle between Saladin's and Richard's forces occurred at the city of Jaffa in July 1192. Saladin took the city, but Richard swiftly captured it from him, and in the end they signed a truce on September 2. Despite the stories and illustrations depicting the two men in direct combat, Saladin and Richard never met. All of their contact was through Saladin's brother al-Adil (ah-DEEL), who was destined to compete with Saladin's sons to succeed him.

After his death Saladin came to be admired and respected by his own people as well as his enemies.

Saladin's last days

Exhausted by war and his illness, Saladin spent his last winter in Damascus. He had not designated a successor, in part because he considered his second son a more capable leader than his eldest, who would normally have taken his place. He died on March 4, 1193, and immediately thereafter, a civil war broke out between the sons and al-Adil, who emerged victorious in 1201.

Buried in Damascus, Saladin was not immediately recognized as a hero in the Muslim world. In part this was because of the caliphs and others jealous of his position, but in time he would gain wide respect in the lands he had defended. Ironically, his greatest admirers in the time immediately following his death were his former enemies in Europe.

So great was the Europeans' respect for their Muslim foe that some of them suspected he was secretly a Christian. Later **Dante** (see entry), in his *Inferno,* would picture Saladin spending eternity in a place set aside for godly non-Christians.

For More Information

Books

Grousset, René. *The Epic of the Crusades.* Translated by Noël Lindsay. New York: Orion Press, 1970.

Kernaghan, Pamela. *The Crusades: Cultures in Conflict.* New York: Cambridge University Press, 1993.

Kuskin, Karla. *Jerusalem, Shining Still.* Illustrations by David Frampton. New York: Harper & Row, 1987.

Martell, Hazel. *The Normans.* New York: New Discovery Books, 1992.

Rice, Chris and Melanie Rice. *Crusades: The Battle for Jerusalem.* New York: DK Publishing, 2000.

Walker, Kathrine Sorley. *Saladin: Sultan of the Holy Sword.* London: Dobson, 1971.

Web Sites

"The Fall of Jerusalem, 1099." [Online] Available http://www.hillsdale. edu/dept/History/Documents/War/Med/Crusade/1099-Jerusalem. htm (last accessed July 26, 2000).

"First Crusade." [Online] Available http://members.xoom.com/_XMCM/ doru_gavril/crusadegen.htm (last accessed July 26, 2000).

"A History and Mythos of the Knights Templar—Saladin." [Online] Available http://intranet.ca/~magicworks/knights/saladin.html (last accessed July 26, 2000).

"ORB—Crusades." *ORB: The Online Reference Book for Medieval Studies.* [Online] Available http://orb.rhodes.edu/encyclop/religion/crusades/ Crusade_Intro.html (last accessed July 26, 2000).

"Saladin." [Online] Available http://i-cias.com/e.o/saladin.htm (last accessed July 26, 2000).

Shotoku Taishi

Born 573
Died 621

Japanese prince and regent

Like **Clovis** in France (see entry) and Toghril Beg in Turkey (see box), the Japanese prince Shotoku Taishi (shoh-TOH-koo ty-EE-shee) can rightly be called "the father of his country." As regent or advisor to the empress, he held the true political power in Japan, and exercised it to initiate a series of reforms that affected virtually every aspect of Japanese life.

In the realm of law and government, Shotoku is credited as the author of the "Seventeen-Article Constitution," a document that provided the governing principles of Japanese society. These principles were a combination of Japan's native Shinto religion and two belief systems, Buddhism and Confucianism, imported from China. The widespread acceptance of those "foreign" ideas, and their incorporation into Japanese culture, can largely be attributed to Shotoku, who remains one of Japan's most highly esteemed historical figures.

Buddhism and other Chinese influences

Japan had been inhabited for thousands of years before it emerged as a unified nation under the leadership of

"The emperor of the country where the sun rises addresses a letter to the emperor of the country where the sun sets."

Opening lines of first Japanese diplomatic message to China, c. 607

Portrait: Shotoku Taishi (center).

the Yamato (yuh-MAH-toh; "imperial") family during the Kofun period (250–552). The country's actual written history began, however, in 405, when the Japanese adopted the Chinese written language, which they would use for many centuries before developing a version more suited to the Japanese spoken language.

The influence of China, a much older and at that time more advanced civilization, was strong from the beginning. So, too, was the influence of Korea, which in addition to its own traditions had incorporated many aspects of Chinese civilization. One of these was the religion of Buddhism, which first arrived in Japan when the king of Korea sent a set of Buddhist scrolls and an image of the Buddha to the Japanese imperial court in 552.

The Buddha, or Siddhartha Gautama (si-DAR-tuh GOW-tuh-muh), had originated the religion in India more than a thousand years earlier; but as it made its way northward and eastward, the form of Buddhism had changed considerably to accommodate the new lands where it was received. Nonetheless, many in the Japanese ruling classes reacted against the new religion, which they considered a threat to the traditional Japanese faith of Shinto. Prince Shotoku Taishi, a powerful member of the imperial court, would exert the deciding influence, however, helping to incorporate Buddhism into the Japanese way of life.

Regent to the empress

As is the case with many leaders who seem larger than life in retrospect, Shotoku's biography is filled with stories that can only be described as legends. For instance, the *Nihon shoki,* Japan's first important work of history, reports that his mother gave birth to him without labor pains. This story was probably adapted from tales concerning the Buddha's birth; and as with the Buddha, it was said that the young prince—whose name was originally Umayado—could speak from birth.

It is known that Shotoku was the son of the emperor Tachibana and the princess Anahobe (ah-nah-HOH-bee), but other than that, few facts about his early life are clear. The first relatively certain date in Shotoku's personal history was

593. The year before, the emperor Sushun had been murdered by a member of the powerful Soga clan, and in 593 he was replaced by the empress Suiko (soo-EE-koh; ruled 593–628), Shotoku's aunt.

The Japanese emperors and empresses possessed plenty of outward symbols of power, as the splendor of their courts illustrated; but there have been very few imperial leaders in Japanese history who possessed *actual* power. The real influence lay in the position of regent, a person who rules in place of the emperor, and Shotoku's career began when his aunt bestowed on him this distinguished office.

Shotoku's reforms

Among the many reforms initiated by Shotoku was the elevation of the emperor to the role of a god, or *kami;* but again, this was only symbolic, rather than real, power. His association of divine and imperial roles was but one of the many ideas Shotoku borrowed from China, in the process adapting them to Japan's own culture.

Shotoku extended the influence both of Buddhism and of Confucianism. The latter was the system of thought developed by the Chinese scholar Confucius (551–479 B.C.), who emphasized social harmony and respect for authorities. Out of the Confucian system in China had grown an extensive civil service—that is, a network of government officials—and Shotoku adopted these concepts as well.

In 604, Shotoku established his "Seventeen-Article Constitution." A constitution is a written document containing the laws of a nation, and is typically divided into articles,

Toghril Beg

Toghril Beg (tawg-REEL; c. 990–1063) founded the Seljuk dynasty, the first Turkish ruling house to conquer the land today known as Turkey. Until Toghril's time, the region was known as Anatolia, and was part of the Byzantine Empire.

The term "Turk" describes a number of related peoples who came from a region in Central Asia to the north and west of China. They began moving westward in the 500s, and by the 900s the Seljuks—named after Toghril's grandfather—had emerged as a particularly powerful Turkish nation.

In 1040, Toghril helped his brother conquer what is now Afghanistan, but he kept moving westward into Anatolia. By 1040, he had conquered large areas of what is now Turkey—much to the chagrin of the Byzantines, who hoped to drive them out.

But the Seljuks were there to stay, and by 1060 Toghril had assumed leadership over most of the Muslim world. Seljuk power declined in the 1200s, and the Seljuks were later replaced by the long-lasting Ottoman Empire.

or individual statements of principle. Shotoku's constitution, however, is quite different from those used by nations such as the United States in modern times.

Though the constitution had the force of law, its text reads more like a set of guidelines as to how the people should live their lives. The opening statement, which embodied Confucian principles, set the tone: "Harmony is to be valued, and an avoidance of wanton opposition to be honored." The constitution also condemned vices such as gluttony, envy, and flattery.

Land of the Rising Sun

It is fitting that as father of his country, Shotoku would be credited with coining the phrase by which Japan is known throughout the world: "Land of the Rising Sun." A form of that expression appeared in the opening lines of a diplomatic letter sent to China, apparently under Shotoku's authorship, in about 607. Later the Chinese would call the country to the east *Jihpen,* meaning "origins of the sun."

That diplomatic letter served as an introduction for a group of diplomats sent from Japan to China. This mission was a symbol that Japan had arrived, and that it was prepared to initiate contact with the most powerful and influential land in all of East Asia. Many Japanese would remain wary of Chinese ways, however, fearful that these would dilute traditional Japanese beliefs; but Shotoku was not one of the fearful ones.

Leaving his mark

Shotoku, who built many Buddhist temples—including one at Horyuji (HOHR-yoo-jee), built in 607, that is the world's oldest wooden structure—left his mark both literally and figuratively on Japan. Symbolic of the strong impression made by the seventh-century prince is the fact that in modern times his face appears on the widely circulated 10,000-yen note (equivalent to about $75 today).

As with the beginning of his life, little is known about the end. In his last years, he was working on a national history, which may have provided an early source for the *Nihon shoki.*

For More Information

Books

Baralt, Luis A. *Turkey.* New York: Children's Press, 1997.

Dahl, Michael. *Japan.* Mankato, MN: Bridgestone Books, 1997.

Dijkstra, Henk, editor. *History of the Ancient & Medieval World,* Volume 11: *Empires of the Ancient World.* New York: Marshall Cavendish, 1996.

Lyle, Garry. *Turkey.* Philadelphia: Chelsea House Publishers, 1999.

Pilbeam, Mavis. *Japan: 5000 B.C.–Today.* New York: Franklin Watts, 1988.

Sheehan, Sean. *Turkey.* New York: Marshall Cavendish, 1994.

Web Sites

Internet East Asian History Sourcebook. [Online] Available http://www.fordham.edu/halsall/eastasia/eastasiasbook.html (last accessed July 26, 2000).

"The Japanese Constitution." [Online] Available http://www.wsu.edu:8080/~dee/ANCJAPAN/CONST.HTM (last accessed July 26, 2000).

"The Seljuk Civilization." [Online] Available http://www.ekoltravel.com/html/selcuk.htm (last accessed July 26, 2000).

"Seljuq Period 1089–1210." [Online] Available http://www.geocities.com/Athens/5246/Seljuq.html (last accessed July 26, 2000).

T'ai Tsung

Born 599
Died 649

**Chinese emperor,
co-founder of the T'ang dynasty**

Along with his father, T'ai Tsung is credited as the co-founder of the T'ang dynasty (618–907), one of China's greatest ruling houses. The T'ang were noted for the fairness of their government, which contrasted with the more authoritarian region of the preceding Sui dynasty. Under T'ang rule, China's borders reached their greatest extent in history up to that time, and approached the Confucian model of peace and harmony that the Chinese had long prized.

The founding of the T'ang dynasty

Chinese emperors are known by a title assigned only after their death; thus during his lifetime, T'ai Tsung (dy-DZAWNG) was known as Li Shih-min (ZHUR-min). His father, Li Yüan (yee-WAHN; 565–635) would reign from 618 to 626 as the first T'ang (TAHNG) emperor, Kao Tsu (gow-DZÜ).

Ten years before the birth of T'ai Tsung, Yang Chien (also known by his reign title, **Wen Ti**; see entry) ended centuries of chaos in China by founding the Sui (SWEE) dynasty, in which Li Yüan served as an official. The Li family, like

> "If I diminish expenses, lighten the taxes, employ only honest officials, so that the people have clothing enough, that will do more to abolish robbery than the employment of the severest punishments."
>
> *Statement to his ministers*

many Chinese, embraced the principles of Confucianism, a belief system with roots in ancient times that stressed respect for persons in authority. In spite of this, Li Yüan and his sons would lead a revolt against the rule of Yang Chien's son Yang Ti (DEE), who ruled from 604 to 618.

A military governor assigned to protect China's borders against the Turks in the north, Li Yüan formed an alliance with these one-time enemies and marched on the Sui capital at Ch'ang-an, known today as Xian (shee-AHN), in 617. He proclaimed a new dynasty, and became ruler in the following year. By then he was in his early fifties, and he designated his eldest son Li Chien-ch'eng as his heir. His second son, however, had other plans.

T'ai Tsung establishes his rule

That second son was T'ai Tsung, who in 624 led a brilliant operation against another Turkish group—the eastern Turks, not the allies who had helped them come to power. T'ai Tsung next turned on his brothers, arranging an ambush in which both Li Chien-ch'eng and a younger brother, Li Yüan-chi, were killed.

It appears that the father made little effort to stop T'ai Tsung's rise to power, and soon the father became the next target. In 626, T'ai Tsung forced him to abdicate, or step down from the throne, and the reign of T'ai Tsung began in January of the following year. Li Yüan or Kao Tsu lived eight more years, but he no longer held power.

An efficient civil service

Despite the treachery that brought him to power—and in spite of his personality, which was haughty and quick to anger—T'ai Tsung proved a just and fair ruler. His father had already instituted a series of reforms and continued others from the Sui era, and T'ai Tsung greatly expanded the scope of those reforms.

A cornerstone of Sui and T'ang rule was its three-part administrative system, with the government divided into branches for making, reviewing, and carrying out policy. T'ai Tsung allowed the review board and policy-making branches to give input on his decisions and make suggestions, an unusual step in a country where emperors enjoyed near-absolute power.

In line with his Confucian upbringing, which placed a strong emphasis on the role of civil servants or government workers, T'ai Tsung made sure to surround himself with highly capable men. He even hired officials who had served his former rivals, and took steps to ensure that advancement was on the basis of merit and ability, not family relations or social standing.

As a consequence, the T'ang government was one of the most efficient the world has ever known. T'ai Tsung placed monitoring stations along the highways and waterways of the empire, and there officials oversaw taxation, reviewed local grievances, policed commercial activities, and even provided accommodations for travelers.

A flourishing empire

Aware that the people of China had long suffered under oppressive government, T'ai Tsung made land reforms, redistributing property to reflect changes in the size of peasant families. In some areas he reduced taxes, and though taxes on farmers remained high, the peasants began to feel a sense of ownership over their lands, since T'ai Tsung's reforms had seen to it that their property could no longer be seized by feudal lords.

As a result of these reforms, the economy of T'ang China thrived, and economic exchanges with other lands increased. Technology flourished as well, as the Chinese made improvements in printing and paper production. The T'ang government also greatly extended the canal network put in place by the Sui, thus aiding the transport of goods from north to south in a land where most major rivers flowed eastward.

Two Other Dynasties, Two Other Families

A dynasty is a group of people, usually but not always a family, which maintains power over a period of time, and China's history before the twentieth century is divided according to dynasty. During the Middle Ages, the country had five notable dynasties: the Sui (589–618), founded by Wen Ti; the T'ang (618–907), of which T'ai Tsung was a co-founder; the Sung (SOONG; 960–1279); the Mongol-dominated Yüan (1264–1368), founded by **Kublai Khan** (see entry); and the Ming (1368–1644).

In most cases a single family maintained power throughout a given dynasty— yet the name of the ruling house was seldom the same as that of the family: for example, the controlling family of the Sung dynasty was named Chao (ZHOW). The founder, born Chao K'uang-yin (KWAHNG-yin; 927–976), was a military leader whose troops declared him emperor in 960.

Like many dynasties before, the Sung were faced constantly with enemies at their borders. For the most part they dealt with this problem by paying tribute, or money, to hostile forces. This tribute proved costly, and the powerful minister Wang An-shih (1021–1086) put in place a set of reforms to deal with the economic problems caused by the situation.

Wang An-shih arranged loans to farmers, established pay for government labor (which had been infrequent before his time), and reorganized the system of property taxes to make them more fair. This put him on a collision course with another key official, **Ssu-ma Kuang** (see Historians entry), who favored the old way of doing things. The two men remained in conflict for much of their lives, and represented two opposing forces in Chinese government.

Thanks in large part to Wang An-shih, the Sung developed a government at least as efficient as that of the T'ang, but unwise foreign policy decisions forced the tenth Sung emperor, Chao Kou (1107–1187) to move the capital to southern China in 1127. This latter phase of the

Having built his power through the military, as ruler T'ai Tsung established a reputation as a scholar and a patron of the arts and sciences. During his reign and afterward, the arts flourished, and the T'ang dynasty became memorable for the many painters, poets, and philosophers it produced. It also marked a high point in historical scholarship, and T'ai Tsung encouraged the writing of several histories chronicling dynasties up to his own time.

Sung dynasty is known as the Southern Sung, and despite the problems with which China was faced, it saw a great flowering in culture and the arts. Ultimately, however, the Sung would succumb to Mongol invasion, which brought an end to the reign of the eighteenth Sung emperor, Chao Ping (1271–1279), an eight-year-old boy killed by the Mongols.

The Yüan dynasty marked the first time China had been ruled by foreigners, and the Chinese chafed under Mongol rule, biding their time until a strong enough leader rose to overthrow them. That leader was Chu Yüan-chang (ZHÜ yü-AHN-zhang; 1328–1398), an extraordinary man: born a peasant, he became a Buddhist monk before joining a rebel army and ultimately establishing a dynasty that would rule for more than 250 years.

Few of his descendants, however, were his equal—except Chu Ti, better known by his reign title of Yung-lo (1360–1424). Yung-lo sent a series of naval expeditions under the command of Cheng Ho (see box in Henry the Navigator entry) to lands as far away as East Africa, and in 1421 moved the capital from Nanjing (nahn-ZHEENG) in the interior to Beijing (bay-ZHEENG) on the coast. At Beijing, which remains the Chinese capital today, he built a palace five miles in circumference, containing some 2,000 rooms where more than 10,000 servants attended the imperial family. This palace came to be known as the "Forbidden City," meaning that only the emperor and the people directly around him were allowed to enter.

Built to illustrate the boundless extent of Ming power, the Forbidden City became—aside from the Great Wall—the best-known symbol of China in the eyes of the world. However, the costs associated with its construction, as well as other ambitious projects under Yung-lo's reign, weakened the Ming dynasty. Like the T'ang and Sung before it, and indeed like most dynasties in Chinese history, the Ming's brief days of glory would be followed by a long period of decline.

Expansion of China's boundaries

Whereas China had often been cut off to outside influences, under T'ai Tsung's rule a number of foreigners settled within the empire. They brought with them new religions, some of which were previously unknown in China. Buddhism, introduced from India centuries before, was allowed to spread. Likewise the Chinese were exposed to faiths of even

The imperial palace known as the Forbidden City was built during the Ming dynasty, almost 800 years after T'ai Tsung's death. *Reproduced by permission of Susan D. Rock.*

more distant origin: Islam, Zoroastrianism, Manichaeism, Nestorian Christianity, and even Judaism.

Foreign settlement went hand-in-hand with expansion of China's boundaries. On the one hand, T'ai Tsung centralized the government, meaning that he brought as much power under his control as possible. But by filling key government positions with men from various places around the empire, he ensured stability among the various peoples under Chinese rule. This in turn gave him a free hand to undertake several successful military operations against enemies on the borders.

In 630 T'ai Tsung drove out the eastern Turks, against whom he had earlier distinguished himself in battle. He then turned against a western group of Turks, some of his father's former allies, forcing them westward toward Persia and thus opening up the Silk Road, an important trade route. At the empire's southern borders, he defeated the Tibetans in battle,

Emperor Tenchi and Fujiwara Kamatari

To a lesser extent than China, which influenced it greatly during the early medieval period, Japan was prone to occasional revolts that brought sweeping changes in its power structure. One such revolt occurred in 645, led by Crown Prince Nakano Oe (OH-ee; 626–671) and an influential aristocrat named Nakatomi Kamatari (614–669).

At that time, the Soga clan dominated Japanese affairs, but their power had declined after the time of Prince **Shotoku Taishi** (see entry). Less than a quarter-century after Shotoku's death, the two men saw their opportunity, and conspired to murder the leader of the Sogas. They did not take power immediately, however: only in 662 did Nakano Oe assume the throne as Emperor Tenchi.

His co-conspirator also gained a new name in the course of the revolt: by decree of Emperor Tenchi, Kamatari's family became known as Fujiwara. The real power in Japan usually resided in important figures behind the throne, and for many centuries thereafter, the Fujiwara family would control Japan.

Under Fujiwara Kamatari, as he became known, the imperial government put in place the Taika Reforms (TY-kah). Modeled on the policies of T'ai Tsung and other leaders of T'ang China, the Taika Reforms strengthened the power of the central government and established a system of provincial administrators who answered to the capital. The Fujiwara clan would maintain power for several centuries, until the beginning of the Kamakura period (1185–1333).

then formed an alliance by arranging marriages between Tibetan and T'ang leaders.

The decline of T'ai Tsung and his empire

An operation against Korea in 644 proved less successful, and in coming years T'ai Tsung's successors would try again and again—with varying degrees of success—to subdue Korea. The successes of the T'ang dynasty, however, would continue through the reign of many emperors, including China's sole female ruler, **Wu Ze-tian** (see entry).

Under Wu Ze-tian's grandson, Hsüan Tsung (shwee-AHND-zoong; ruled 712–56), the T'ang dynasty would reach its height, but then it began a slow decline. The causes of this decline included forces from outside—the defeat of the T'ang by Arab armies at Talas in Central Asia—and inside. Most notable among the latter were the palace intrigues and revolts associated with Hsüan Tsung's concubine, Yang Kuei-fei (see box in Irene of Athens entry), and her lover An Lu-shan.

T'ai Tsung's own life would mirror that of the dynasty he founded: in his later years he, like the empire, went into a state of decline. Having spent most of his rule as a careful money manager, in his late forties he became absorbed in the pleasures of imperial life, building palaces and lavishing funds on his wives and even his horses and dogs. Likewise he went against his earlier policy of listening to wise counselors, and often ignored the advice of his trusted government ministers. During the failed campaign against Korea, he contracted a disease, and began to wither away, dying in May 649.

For More Information

Books

Field, Catherine. *China*. Austin, TX: Raintree Steck-Vaughn Publishers, 2000.

Gowen, Herbert H. and Josef W. Hall. *An Outline History of China*. New York: D. Appleton and Company, 1926.

Green, Jen. *Japan*. Austin, TX: Raintree Steck-Vaughn Publishers, 2000.

Heinrichs, Ann. *China*. New York: Children's Press, 1997.

Martell, Hazel. *Imperial China, 221 B.C. to A.D. 1294*. Austin, TX: Raintree Steck-Vaughn Publishers, 1999.

Millar, Heather. *China's Tang Dynasty*. New York: Benchmark Books, 1996.

Web Sites

"Chinese History: The Main Dynasties." *The Chinese Odyssey*. [Online] Available http://library.thinkquest.org/10662/normal_dynasty.htm (last accessed July 26, 2000).

"The Emperor of Japan and the History of the Imperial Household of Japan." [Online] Available http://www.geocities.com/~watanabe_ken/tenno.html (last accessed July 26, 2000).

"Internet Resources: China." [Online] Available http://www.wsu.edu:8080/~dee/CHIINRES.HTM (last accessed July 26, 2000).

Tamerlane

Born 1336
Died 1405

Mongol-Turkic conqueror

Though not related to **Genghis Khan** (see entry), Tamerlane came from similar Central Asian roots and saw himself as a successor to the great conqueror. He set out to build an empire of his own, ravaging an area from modern-day Turkey to India, and from Russia to Syria. Along the way, he left a trail of death and mayhem, and though he made significant cultural contributions in his capital at Samarkand, these were outweighed by the misfortunes he dealt his own fellow Mongols and Muslims.

Mongols and Turks

Tamerlane is actually the name by which he became known to Europeans, who were largely spared the force of his wrath. Actually, his name was Timur (tee-MOOR), and an injury earned him the nickname Timur Lenk or "Timur the Lame," which became Tamerlane in European versions of his story.

He grew up in the region of the Chagatai khanate (chah-guh-TY KAHN-et), which included modern-day Uzbek-

"Timur ... aspired to rival Chinghis [Genghis Khan]. In the extent of his conquests and the ferocity of his behavior, he did; he may even have been as great a leader of men. None the less, he lacked the statesmanship of his predecessors."

J. M. Roberts, The Age of Diverging Traditions

Portrait: *Reproduced by permission of the Library of Congress.*

343

istan and other former Soviet republics in Central Asia. A century before his time, Genghis Khan had conquered the territory, which was named after one of his sons.

Tamerlane, who was born in 1336 near the city of Samarkand (sah-mur-KAHND) in what is now Uzbekistan, descended from the same Mongol stock as Genghis, though they were not related. His lineage was also partly Turkic, reflecting the heritage of other nomadic peoples who had swept over the region in centuries past. As a Muslim, he was thus related by both blood and religion to the Turks of the Ottoman Empire, who would later become some of his many victims.

Winning control of Chagatai

In his early career, Tamerlane developed a reputation as a petty warlord and marauder, and gathered around him a following of loyal men. Beginning in 1361, when he was twenty-five years old, he set out to take advantage of the Mongols' fading control over Chagatai and make himself ruler. At first unsuccessful, he did become recognized as emir (eh-MEER), a Muslim title for a political and military leader, over his own Barlas tribe.

In 1364, Tamerlane allied himself with a neighboring emir, Husayn, and the two set out to win control of the khanate. To seal their alliance, he married one of Husayn's sisters; but soon after the two men conquered Chagatai late in 1364, a power struggle ensued, with Husayn challenging Tamerlane's claims on leadership.

During his military campaigns in this phase, Tamerlane sustained injuries to his right shoulder, hand, and thigh, which resulted in his nickname of "Timur the Lame." It is hard to imagine that anyone dared call him this to his face, because he had already established a reputation as a merciless warlord.

In 1370, Tamerlane killed off Husayn and took four of his wives. One of these was the daughter of a former Chagatai khan, and by marrying her he could finally claim a link to the great Genghis. Thereafter he used the title Kurgan (koor-GAHN), meaning "son-in-law" of the Khan.

Building Samarkand and his empire

Tamerlane did not necessarily care for the trappings of power, as long as he had the real thing, and therefore he continued to rule as emir while a puppet leader held the title of khan. Secure in his control over the khanate, he set about turning Samarkand into a glorious capital, building palaces and forts. He also supported the arts in his city, which became a cultural center for the region; but Tamerlane, who was most interested in the art of war, did not stay around to enjoy his city's cultural offerings.

In the 1380s, he set out to conquer neighboring lands, including what is now Afghanistan, much of Persia (modern Iran), Azerbaijan, and Kurdistan, a mountainous region that runs from Turkey to Iran in the north. He was methodical in building his empire: in each new region, he would demand that the local rulers submit, and if they refused, he would deal them such a severe blow that they eventually relented.

The Ulug Bek madrasah in Samarkand, Uzbekistan. Tamerlane established Samarkand as the glorious capital of his empire. *Photograph by Charlotte Kahler. Reproduced by permission of Charlotte Kahler Stock Photography.*

Vlad Tepes

Depending on what side one happened to be on, Tamerlane was either a great hero or a criminal and a murderer. To an even greater extent, this was true of Vlad Tepes (VLAHD TSEH-pesh; c. 1431–1476), sometimes known as Vlad the Impaler. Vlad was the prince of Walachia (wuh-LAYK-ee-uh) in what is now Romania, and his father was a man so cruel he was nicknamed "the Devil," or Vlad Dracul (drah-KOOL). Together the two formed the basis for the Dracula legend, popularized by Bram Stoker's 1897 novel *Dracula,* and by countless movies.

Caught in the middle of a struggle between Hungarian and Turkish forces, Vlad Tepes at first aligned himself with the Turks before changing sides to support the Hungarians in 1456. His actions over the next six years earned him a reputation as a dedicated freedom fighter in some quarters; more people, however, chose to view him as what in modern times would be called a homicidal maniac.

Declaring war on the Germans, also a force in the region, Vlad set out on a campaign of wholesale slaughter in which thousands of men, women, and children in the region of Transylvania died. Vlad's chosen instruments of murder were long stakes with which he and his soldiers skewered, or impaled, the bodies of their victims; hence his nickname.

By 1462, his own nobles had had enough of Vlad, and they deposed him. He escaped to Hungary, where his former allies—no doubt afraid of what he might do to *them*—placed him under house arrest. He lived that way for twelve years; then he returned to Walachia, only to be killed shortly afterward in battle. After his death, legends of his cruelty circulated, and as the tale changed hands, newer and more ghastly dimensions were added, including tales that Vlad drank blood. In time the myth would obscure the reality of Vlad's actual career, which was gruesome enough.

The Golden Horde

Tamerlane's goal seems to have been to plunge into Anatolia (now Turkey), but in the mid-1380s he was diverted by affairs to the north. One of his former associates had gained control of the Golden Horde, as the vast Mongol lands in Russia were called. He then began threatening Tamerlane's newly acquired lands in Iran and the Caucasus (a region to the south of Russia, including Azerbaijan, Armenia, and Georgia).

Forced to return to his home base to defend it, in 1390 Tamerlane defeated his enemies in the Golden Horde.

This would lead to their permanent weakening, and a century later, the Russians would destroy the last remnants of their former rulers' empire. As for Tamerlane, in 1392 he began a new phase of conquest known as the Five Years' Campaign, in which he subdued virtually all of Iran.

Wide-ranging campaigns

One reason why Tamerlane's conquests did not last far beyond his lifetime was the fact that he seldom stayed in one place long enough to consolidate his rule. He would rush into an area, savage it, and then plunge off in a completely different direction, almost literally to the other end of the known world.

In 1398 he advanced on India, burning and looting the city of Delhi, but a year later he was in Syria, fighting against the Turkish Mamluks (mam-LOOKZ) and Ottomans. The Mamluks controlled Egypt, and the more powerful Ottomans held a large empire centered on Turkey. In 1402, he did battle with forces commanded by the Ottoman sultan Bajazed (by-yuh-ZEED). Tamerlane captured Bajazed and held him for ransom, but the ruler was so humiliated that he committed suicide.

Rather than stay in Turkey and win more territory, Tamerlane headed east again to Samarkand in 1404. He rested up for a few months, then in the fall moved out again, this time with an even more ambitious plan in mind: the conquest of China. On the way, however, he became ill, and died in February 1405 at the age of sixty-nine.

As could have been predicted, the aftermath of Tamerlane's rule saw the loss of many territories by his successors. Nonetheless, years later, a descendant named Babur (BAH-boor, "Lion"; 1483–1530) would establish a long-lasting dynasty in India.

For More Information

Books

Boardman, Fon Wyman, Jr. *Tyrants and Conquerors*. New York: H. Z. Walck, 1977.

Roberts, J. M. *The Illustrated History of the World,* Volume 4: *The Age of Diverging Traditions.* New York: Oxford, 1998.

Streissguth, Thomas. *Legends of Dracula.* Minneapolis, MN: Lerner Publications, 1999.

Wepman, Dennis. *Tamerlane.* New York: Chelsea House Publishers, 1987.

Web Sites

"Cyberiran: Invasions of the Mongols and Tamerlane." *Cyberiran.* [Online] Available http://www.cyberiran.com/history/invasion/shtml (last accessed July 26, 2000).

"Dracula: The Real Story." [Online] Available http://www.geocities.com/Athens/Atrium/1233/dracula/ (last accessed July 26, 2000).

The History of the Family Dracul. [Online] Available http://www.opa.com/vampire/Dracula.html (last accessed July 26, 2000).

Miller, Elizabeth. "Dracula: The History of Myth and the Myth of History." [Online] Available http://www.ucs.mun.ca/~emiller/vladjotd.htm (last accessed July 26, 2000).

"Uzbekistan: The Rule of Timur." [Online] Available http://lcweb2.loc.gov/cgi-bin/query/r?frd/cstdy:@field(DOCID+uz0018) (last accessed July 26, 2000).

Thomas Aquinas

Born c. 1225
Died 1274

Italian philosopher and theologian

The writings of Thomas Aquinas represented the pinnacle of the medieval school of thought known as Scholasticism. The latter, which had its roots in the work of **Abelard** (see entry) and others, attempted to bring together Christian faith, classical learning, and knowledge of the world. Thomas Aquinas wrote his *Summa theologica* to address new ideas that seemed to threaten the stability of Christian faith. As an inheritor of the Scholastic tradition, Thomas and his work can be seen on the one hand as the culmination of many centuries of thinking. Yet other ways of looking at the world were also emerging in Thomas's time and afterward, and thus his adherence to the Scholastic line can also be viewed as a defense of an old way of life against change.

The influence of Frederick II

Born of nobility in the Italian town of Aquino—hence his name, Aquinas (uh-KWYN-us)—Thomas was the youngest son of a count who descended from the Normans. His father had once fought in the armies of Emperor **Frederick II** (see

"Human salvation demands the divine disclosure of truths surpassing reason."

Summa theologica

Portrait: *Reproduced by permission of the Corbis Corporation.*

349

Holy Roman Emperors entry), who like many another Holy Roman emperor was in conflict with the reigning pope. Hoping to ensure their good standing with the church, his parents placed the five-year-old Thomas in the Benedictine monastery at Monte Cassino, founded by St. Benedict (see box in Innocent III entry).

Things did not quite work out as planned: the emperor's conflict with the pope led to the latter excommunicating Frederick, or expelling him from the church, in 1239, when Thomas was fourteen. As a result, Frederick threatened Monte Cassino, and Thomas had to change schools. He moved to Naples in southern Italy, where he enrolled in what was to become that city's university.

The university system of Europe was in its earliest days at that time, and a number of new ideas were in the air. Most of these "new" concepts were actually old ones, inherited from the ancient Greeks and translated by Arab thinkers such as **Averroës** (see entry). The latter's writings had a great impact on the school at Naples, not only because it was relatively close to the Arab world, but also because Frederick (who had founded the school in 1224) encouraged the introduction of Islamic as well as Christian ideas there.

Albertus Magnus and the bellowing ox

Though he had been trained as a Benedictine, Thomas found himself drawn by the order founded by St. Dominic (see box in St. Francis of Assisi entry). In 1244, he joined the Dominicans against the protests of his mother, now a widow, and his brothers. The following year found him studying with the Dominicans at the University of Paris, where he came under the influence of Albertus Magnus (c. 1200–1280).

The latter, whose name means "Albert the Great," was considered the greatest scholar of his time, though he has been overshadowed by Thomas, his more famous pupil. Albert made a prophecy about Thomas, who had received the nickname "the dumb ox" from his classmates. Obviously it was an uncomplimentary expression; however, it referred not to Thomas's intellect—which was clearly superior to that of most—but to his physical body, which was tall, fat, and slow.

Albert, however, remarked that the bellow of this ox would be heard around the world.

Begins his life's work

Thomas studied with Albert at the latter's home in Cologne, now a city in western Germany, from 1248 to 1252; then he returned to Paris to earn his degree in theology, or the study of questions relating to God and religion. Like graduate students now, Thomas served as a teacher of undergraduates while earning his own graduate degree; then in 1256, he obtained his license to teach theology as a full-time instructor at the university.

As an undergraduate, Thomas had written a commentary of a kind typical among the works of university students at that time. Next he produced the *Summa contra gentiles* (c. 1258–64), a book designed to aid Dominican missionaries in Spain and North Africa who got into religious arguments with Jews and Muslims, or with Christians who had adopted heretical ideas (ideas contrary to church teachings).

In 1261, Thomas moved to Rome to serve as a lecturer at the papal court, and while there, he began writing his most important work, *Summa theologica* (c. 1265–73). Part one, completed during this time, concerned the existence and attributes, or characteristics, of God. He then returned to Paris, just in time to become involved in a brewing controversy.

Caught in a controversy

The influence of Averroës had become widespread among scholars and students at the University of Paris. The Arab philosopher held the viewpoint that one can use both reason and faith without the two contradicting one another. This could also be interpreted to mean that reason sometimes takes greater importance than religious faith—an idea the church considered dangerous.

Thomas argued against one of the leading promoters of Averroës's ideas, but Thomas too came under suspicion because in his writing he reflected the influence of the ancient Greek philosopher Aristotle. (At that time, church authorities were still skeptical of philosophical ideas that came from the

Some Notable Thinkers and Scholars of the Middle Ages

The pages of medieval history are filled with a number of scholars and thinkers who are noteworthy, even if not well known. An example is Dionysius Exiguus (dy-oh-NISH-us ek-SIJ-yoo-uhs; c. 500–c. 560), a Byzantine monk and scholar from what is now Russia. Though his name is not exactly a household word, perhaps it should be: Dionysius originated the system of dating events from the birth of Christ. Because he miscalculated the date of Christ's birth in relation to the founding of Rome, his system resulted in error, illustrated by the fact that Christ himself was probably born in 6 B.C. Also, Dionysius lacked the concept of zero, meaning that in his system, the next year after 1 B.C. was A.D. 1. For this reason, as a number of commentators noted in 1999 and years following, the third millennium began not on January 1, 2000, but on January 1, 2001.

Another fascinating figure was Isidore of Seville (c. 560–636), a Spanish priest who wrote a number of encyclopedic works. Isidore was considered one of the most learned men of his time, and the fact that his writings are filled with myths and superstitions says a great deal about the poor quality of learning in the early Middle Ages.

Soon after Isidore's time, Spain was overrun by Muslims, and this ironically made it a center for Jewish culture and scholarship. Among the important Jewish intellectual figures produced by Muslim Spain was Hisdai ibn Shaprut (kis-DY ib'n shahp-RÜT; c. 915–c. 975), court physician to Caliph Abd ar-Rahman III, whose support of scholarship helped initiate a golden age of Hebrew learning in Spain. One of the beneficiaries of his efforts was Samuel ha-Nagid (hah-NAH-geed; 993–c. 1055), who also held an important position in the Muslim government. Samuel produced a commentary on the Talmud, or Jewish scriptures, that continued to be influential for many years. Shlomo Yitzhaqi (sh'loh-MOH yits-HAHK-y; 1040–1105) also wrote

ancient Greeks, since they were pagans and not Christians.) Thomas did indeed maintain that reason can aid the believer in discovering certain truths about God, an idea he put to use in several proofs of God's existence; but at all times Thomas saw reason as secondary to faith.

Completion of the *Summa theologica*

By 1271 or 1272, Thomas had completed the second portion of his *Summa theologica,* concerning questions of hap-

commentaries on the Talmud. Better known by the nickname Rashi (RAH-shee), this French rabbi was one of the few notable Jewish figures in Christian Europe.

As Europe emerged from the Dark Ages into the gradual rebirth of learning that attended the eleventh century, it produced a number of figures who contributed to literature, philosophy, and the arts. One of these was a woman, Hrotsvitha von Gandersheim (raws-VEE-tah; GAHN-durs-hym; c. 935–1000). Regarded as the first woman to write poetry in German, she helped revive the art of drama, which had been dormant for many years due to its association with pagan Rome. She wrote six comedies based on the work of the ancient Roman playwright Terence, but embodying Christian ideas.

Another notable scholar was a pope, Sylvester II (945–1003; ruled 999–1003), born in France with the name Gerbert. Formerly a teacher, he studied mathematics and the natural sciences, and

wrote a number of works, including textbooks and two books on mathematics. He also influenced young **Otto III** (see Holy Roman Emperors entry) in his dreams of a unified empire.

Among the areas that Gerbert promoted was music, which would be heavily affected by the work of Guido of Arezzo (GWEE-doh; ar-RED-zoh; c. 991–1050). Guido developed the rudiments of the system of musical notation in use today, particularly the four-line staff.

This list of notable scholars began with a Byzantine writer, and ends with one: Michael Psellus (SEL-us; 1018–c. 1078). An important official in the empire's government, he also served as professor of philosophy in Constantinople. Michael was widely known for his encyclopedic knowledge and his promotion of classical studies, particularly those involving the ancient philosopher Plato. His most well known work was the *Chronographia*, a history of the Byzantine Empire from 976 to 1078.

piness, sin, law, and grace. Though he may have moved slowly, he was a man of boundless energy who, it was said, employed as many as four secretaries at a time so that he could dictate to them. The completed *Summa theologica,* the greatest of his books, though only one of several, ran to about two million words—the equivalent of about 8,000 double-spaced, typewritten sheets.

Having returned to Naples in 1272 to set up a Dominican study house attached to the university there, Thomas went to work on the third part of the *Summa,* this one concerning the identity of Christ and the meaning of his work. On December 6, 1273, his own work suddenly stopped, and he explained to others that everything he had done seemed meaningless. Whether he suffered a physical breakdown, experienced a spiritual insight, or simply ran out of ideas is not known.

His health failing, Thomas in 1274 set out to attend a church council in France. He was struck on the head by a branch falling from a tree over the road, and may have suffered a concussion. He stopped at a castle belonging to his niece to recover, and soon afterward was taken to a monastery, where he died on March 7, 1274.

Doctor of the Church

It is ironic that Thomas would later be regarded as a symbol of Catholic rigidity. At the time of his death, his work was under question by the church, which took issue with his attempts to reconcile reason and faith. Four decades later, however, inquiries were under way to canonize him, or declare him a saint. He was canonized in 1323, and in 1567 named a Doctor of the Church, or one of the leading church fathers.

As for the viewpoint that Thomas represented an attempt to hold on the past, this idea fails to take into account the actual conditions of his time. Though forces were at work that would ultimately challenge the absolute power of the church—forces that included the rise of nation-states, international trade, and a growing attitude of scientific curiosity—the church was still very much in control, and it still tended to regard new ideas as heresy. Thus Thomas was very much on the cutting edge when he asserted that it was possible to use reason and still remain firm in dedication to God. Throughout his career, he walked a fine line, and he managed to do so without losing his integrity either as a man of faith or as a thinker.

For More Information

Books

Brehaut, Ernest. *An Encyclopedist of the Dark Ages, Isidore of Seville.* New York: Benjamin Franklin, 1964.

Daughters of St. Paul. *Pillar in the Twilight: The Life of St. Thomas Aquinas.* Illustrated by the Daughters of St. Paul. Boston: St. Paul Editions, 1967.

Harvey, O. L. *Time Shaper, Day Counter: Dionysius and Scaliger.* Silver Spring, MD: Harvey, 1976.

Pittenger, W. Norman. *Saint Thomas Aquinas: The Angelic Doctor.* New York: Franklin Watts, 1969.

Web Sites

Aquinas Page. [Online] Available http://gsep.pepperdine.edu/gsep/class/ethics/Aquinas/AQHome.html (last accessed July 26, 2000).

"Stephen Loughlin's Home Page—St. Thomas Aquinas." [Online] Available http://www.niagara.edu/~loughlin/ (last accessed July 26, 2000).

"Thomas.htm." [Online] Available http://www.op.org/domcentral/people/vocations/Thomas.htm (last accessed July 26, 2000).

"Tips on Reading Thomas Aquinas." [Online] Available http://www.bluffton.edu/~humanities/1/st_tips.htm (last accessed July 26, 2000).

"The 21st Century and the Third Millennium." [Online] Available http://aa.usno.navy.mil/AA/faq/docs/millennium.html (last accessed July 26, 2000).

Wen Ti

Born 541
Died 604

**Chinese emperor,
founder of Sui dynasty**

Founder of the short-lived Sui dynasty, Wen Ti (or Yang Chien, as he was born) is little known outside of China, but he was a highly important figure in that nation's history. He re-unified the empire after three centuries of chaos, establishing a strong central government and a set of reforms that paved the way for the T'ang dynasty of **T'ai Tsung** (see entry). Wen Ti was also a ruthless figure, a man who did not shrink back from killing his own grandson, and as a leader he was equally severe.

Seizing power over the Chou

In many ways, China can be compared to the Roman Empire. As Rome had flourished under strong rulers during ancient times, China reached a height of unity and order under the Han (HAHN) dynasty, established in 207 B.C. But whereas Rome began a long, slow decline in the third century A.D., China entered a period of outright disorder or anarchy following the downfall of the Han in 220.

The man who brought an end to this chaos with the establishment of the Sui dynasty (SWEE) was Yang Chien

(YAHNG jee-AHN), who would be remembered by his reign title of Wen Ti (wun-DEE). He grew up in Chou (ZHOH), one of the many states competing to control northern China. The Chou rulers were not Chinese; they came from the many groups of Turkish and Mongolian peoples who had long threatened China's borders.

Wen Ti's family had served the Chou for many years, and at age sixteen he was married into the Dugu clan, rulers of Chou. He later married off his eldest daughter to the Chou ruler in 578, but soon he turned against his former allies. In 580, his son-in-law died, and Wen Ti took advantage of the situation to seize power. Establishing a pattern that would characterize his later career, Wen Ti executed fifty-nine members of the ruling family, including his own grandson, a potential rival for the Chou throne.

Emperor of China

In 581, Wen Ti declared himself emperor of the Sui dynasty, but the beginning of the Sui period in Chinese history is usually dated at 589. In the intervening years, he defeated the most prominent of the various states vying for power, and made himself ruler of all China.

Haughty and ill-disposed toward criticism, Wen Ti was a severe leader who would send spies to bribe allies, then arrange the murder of those who accepted the bribes. In one of the greatest undertakings of his reign, the building of the Grand Canal, he made use of millions of slave laborers, and the project took an incalculable toll in human lives.

But the Grand Canal, an eleven-hundred-mile waterway that linked the Yellow River in the north with the Yangtze (YAHNG-say) in the south, was crucial to the development of China. In a vast empire where transportation was often difficult and where major rivers flow east and west, the Grand Canal provided an important link that stimulated commerce. Later emperors would continue to make improvements on the canal, which, like the Great Wall of China, was a symbol of the nation's immensity and power.

Wen Ti's reforms

Despite his bad temper and ruthless ways, Wen Ti was a shrewd administrator who ended Chinese disunity by bringing the nation under his centralized control. Whereas the Western Roman Empire had dissolved into many states, he took steps to ensure this did not happen in China, bringing local leaders into his government and thus under his sway.

Wen Ti also caused a revival of China's age-old civil service system—that is, its efficient network of government officials. The latter was built on the principles of Confucius (551–479 B.C.), a philosopher who taught principles of social harmony and respect for persons in authority.

In line with Confucian beliefs, Wen Ti restored an old form of land redistribution called the "equal-field" system: he took power from local landlords, increasing his standing among China's many peasants by parcelling out land to them. T'ai Tsung and the other T'ang rulers would later adopt and expand the equal-field system.

Foreign wars

China had always been faced by challenges at its borders, particularly in the north, where the Turks dominated. With regard to the Turks, Wen Ti had a stroke of good fortune: the two most powerful Turkish tribes fell into conflict soon after he took power, and he was able to successfully play each side against the other.

He was not so successful in Korea, a land the Han dynasty had formerly controlled. Wen Ti would be the first of many leaders who tried and failed to bring the neighboring country back under Chinese rule. In all, he and his son, Yang Ti (YAHNG), launched three campaigns against Korea, and each failed.

Yang Ti and the end of the dynasty

The costs of the Korean campaigns, both in terms of money and manpower, eroded Wen Ti's standing with his people. Problems at home did not become unmanageable, however, until the reign of Yang Ti, who assumed the throne

People Who Took Power from Outside

In 1388, a Korean general named Yi Song-gye (sawng-GYAY) staged an armed revolt and seized control of his country, establishing a dynasty that would last until 1910. He was just one of many figures who, like Wen Ti, came from outside the centers of power and assumed control. Other outsiders were not as successful.

T'ang dynasty China endured two major revolts, the first led by An Lu-shan (ahn loo-SHAHN; 703–757). Despite his "foreign" heritage—he was born of mixed Turkish and Iranian descent—the young general rose through the ranks, and became a favorite of T'ang emperor Hsüan Tsung (shwee-AHND-zoong; ruled 712–56). He also became a favorite, and perhaps a lover, of the emperor's beloved concubine Yang Kuei-fei (see box in Irene of Athens entry). Taking advantage of weakened T'ang power following a defeat by Arab forces in 751, An Lu-shan led a rebellion in 755, and declared himself emperor of the "Great Yen" dynasty. In the end, he was betrayed by his son, who had him murdered. Some 130 years later, a salt smuggler named Huang Ch'ao (hwahng CHOW) formed a rebel band and captured several key cities. He, too, declared a new dynasty, the Ta Ch'i, but in 883 he was captured and executed. His revolt hastened the downfall of the T'ang in 907.

The Crusades (1095–1291) produced their own varieties of "outsider" movements, among them the Peasants' Crusade of 1096–97. Its leaders were two Frenchmen, a monk named Peter the Hermit (c. 1050–1105) and a "knight" who called himself Gautier Sans Avoir (GOH-tee-ay SAWNZ a-VWAH, "Walter the Penniless"). They led mobs of poor people on crusades to the Holy Land before the official troops of the First Crusade even left Europe. The peasants were no match for the Turkish troops they faced in Anatolia, and most of them (Gautier included) died in the fighting. Peter, who happened to be away in Constantinople, lived to join in the conquest of Jerusalem, and spent his last years quietly as a monk in Belgium.

Around the same time as the Peasants' Crusade, a more sinister force

after Wen Ti's death in 604. (Some historians believe Yang Ti poisoned his sixty-three-year-old father.)

Yang Ti mirrored his father in his efforts to expand the country's network of canals, and in his successful military campaigns in Vietnam and Central Asia. But by the time he launched a new military operation against the Koreans in 612, unrest at home was growing. Six years later, in 618, Yang

was forming on the Muslim side. These were the Assassins, founded in 1090 by a radical Iranian religious leader named Hasan-e Sabbah (khah-SAHN-uh shuh-BAH; died 1124). Hasan and his followers seized a mountain fortress and there trained killers to eliminate leaders they hated—both Muslims and Christians. Crusaders later brought the word "assassin" home with them, and eventually it became a term for a politically motivated murderer.

By the mid-1300s, the Crusades had ended in failure, and Europe was consumed by the Black Death, or Plague, which in four years killed more Europeans—around thirty million—than all medieval wars combined. The Plague had many side effects, including a decrease in the work force, and as a result, peasants and the working class began demanding higher wages. The rich responded by using their political power to force a freeze on pay increases, and by 1381 the poor in England revolted. They chose Wat Tyler, who may have gotten his name because he made tiles, as their leader, and he presented a set of demands to King Richard II. Richard was willing to take the peasants and workers seriously, but he was only fourteen years old, and his advisors prevailed. Wat Tyler was murdered on June 15, 1381, by government forces.

In the year the Plague began, 1347, Cola di Rienzo (RYENT-soh; 1313–1354) overthrew the government in Rome and announced that he would restore the glory of Rome's former days. He even gave himself the ancient Roman title of tribune, but he ruled as harshly as a bad Roman emperor, and was expelled in 1348. Six years later, he returned to power, but was soon murdered in a riot. His story inspired nineteenth-century German composer Richard Wagner (REE-kard VAHG-nur) to write an opera about him. Later, dictator Adolf Hitler would say that he conceived his life's mission—ultimately, the founding of the Nazi state and killing of six million Jews—during a performance of Wagner's *Rienzi*.

Ti was assassinated, and the T'ang dynasty replaced the Sui after just twenty-nine years.

Ch'in and Sui

Wen Ti has often been compared to Ch'in Shih Huang Ti (shee-HWAHNG-tee; 259–210 B.C.). The latter was China's first emperor and the builder of the Great Wall. His impact on the nation can be judged by the fact that the name "China" is taken from that of his dynasty, the Ch'in (221–207 B.C.).

Both Wen Ti and Shih Huang Ti were ruthless men who overcame many competitors to place the nation under their sole rule. Both instigated vast public works projects, and both gave the nation much-needed unity—though at the cost of enormous suffering. Due to the cruelty of their leaders, both the Sui and Ch'in dynasties would end quickly, in both cases with the overthrow of the founder's son. But both also made possible the achievements of later dynasties, the Han and T'ang, respectively.

For More Information

Books

Bradford, Karleen. *There Will Be Wolves* (fiction about Peter the Hermit). New York: Lodestar Books, 1996.

Branford, Henrietta. *Fire, Bed, and Bone* (fiction about Wat Tyler). Cambridge, MA: Candlewick Press, 1998.

Corn, Kahane and Jacki Moline. *Madcap Men and Wacky Women from History.* New York: J. Messner, 1987.

Landau, Elaine. *Korea.* New York: Children's Press, 1999.

Percival, Yonit and Alastair Percival. *The Ancient Far East.* Vero Beach, FL: Rourke Enterprises/Marshall Cavendish, 1988.

Web Sites

"Ancient China: The Sui." [Online] Available http://www.wsu.edu:8080/~dee/CHEMPIRE/SUI.HTM (last accessed July 26, 2000).

"The History of the 1381 Peasants' Rebellion." [Online] Available http://otal.umd.edu/~mhill/wathistory.htm (last accessed July 26, 2000).

"Ill-Fated Crusade of the Poor People." *Military History.* [Online] Available http://www.thehistorynet.com/MilitaryHistory/articles/1998/0298_text.htm (last accessed July 26, 2000).

"Lady Godiva." [Online] Available http://www.abacom.com/~jkrause/godiva.html (last accessed July 26, 2000).

"Lady Godiva." [Online] Available http://www.eliki.com/realms/charna/godiva.html (last accessed July 26, 2000).

"Medieval Sourcebook: Anonimalle Chronicle: English Peasants' Revolt 1381." *Medieval Sourcebook.* [Online] Available http://www.fordham.edu/halsall/source/anon1381.html (last accessed July 26, 2000).

"Overview of Korea." [Online] Available http://loki.stockton.edu/~gilmorew/consorti/1deasia.htm (last accessed July 26, 2000).

"Sui Dynasty." [Online] Available http://library.thinkquest.org/12255/library/dynasty/sui.html (last accessed July 26, 2000).

William the Conqueror

Born c. 1027
Died 1087

Norman king of England

William I, better known as William the Conqueror, was an illegitimate child who grew up to become one of the most powerful men in Western Europe. In 1066, he launched an invasion of England and gained control after defeating King Harold at the Battle of Hastings.

The victory of William and the Normans forever changed the character of England. He instituted new laws and greatly increased the power of English kings over noblemen. He also initiated a new line of English royalty, and even today the British royal house is distantly related to William. But the greatest mark on history left by William came with the influence of the Normans on aspects of English life ranging from architecture to language.

William's beginnings

The ancestors of William's father, Duke Robert I of Normandy, were Vikings or "Northmen"; hence the name they took on when they settled in France: Normans.

"He was great in body and strong, tall in stature but not ungainly."

The monk of Caen

Portrait: *Reproduced by permission of the Library of Congress.*

William's mother, Herleve (ur-LEV), was French, the daughter of a tanner. As their name implied, tanners were responsible for tanning cowhides, work which usually involved treating the leather with cow's urine. It was not a very pleasant background, but the fact that William was illegitimate (i.e., his parents were not married) was far more unpleasant in the eyes of his neighbors. It would be years before he gained full acceptance within the community.

Duke Robert and Herleve had another child, a girl named Adelaide, and later Robert arranged for Herleve to marry a powerful nobleman, with whom she had two sons, Odo and Robert. These two half-brothers of William would later play an important role in his career. Duke Robert went on to marry the sister of Canute, Danish king of England (ruled 1016–35), but the marriage did not produce any children. In 1035, he went on a pilgrimage to Jerusalem, and before leaving he convinced the nobles within the duchy (an area ruled by a duke) of Normandy to recognize William as his legitimate heir.

As it turned out, Duke Robert died on the return trip. William was only seven or eight at the time, and the next years were difficult ones as he attempted to maintain control over Normandy. Both men appointed to act as his guardians and advisors were killed, but by the age of fifteen William, recently knighted, had emerged as a powerful force in his own right.

Securing his power

William survived a rebellion in 1046, when he was about nineteen, and proved his abilities as a leader; therefore King Henry I of France asked for his help in a 1051 campaign. According to the feudal system, William's people owed him their loyalty in exchange for his protection, and likewise William owed the king his loyalty in exchange for Henry's protection. William won the king's favor by serving him well, but their relations would sour later, when William's power threatened to overshadow that of the king.

William assisted Henry in subduing Geoffrey Martel, count of Anjou (ahn-ZHOO), and conducted a successful siege, or attack, on a city controlled by Geoffrey. The people of the city taunted William by hanging out hides from the town walls bearing the insult "Hides for the tanner!" Angered, William destroyed the city and executed many of its citizens. Geoffrey fled for his life.

Recognizing that his illegitimacy would be a continuing source of challenges to his authority, William made up his mind to marry well. After years of careful negotiations, in 1052 or 1053 he married Matilda of Flanders. Despite the fact that the marriage had complex but highly significant political reasons behind it, it appears that it was a happy one. They must have made a strange-looking couple, since William was a large man and Matilda stood only four feet tall, but together they had four sons and five or six daughters.

Eyes on England

By the early 1060s, a number of things were falling into line for William. In 1060, both King Henry and Geoffrey of Anjou died, removing two possible opponents. At the same time, William enjoyed good relations with the powerful Catholic Church, which gave its blessing to his next project—the most important one of his life.

For a long time, it had appeared that England was up for grabs, as the power of its Anglo-Saxon kings began to fade. The Normans had first established a foothold there in 1002, when Emma of Normandy married King Ethelred the Unready. Their half-Norman son Edward the Confessor became king in 1042, and when he died in early January 1066, many Normans took this as a sign that the time had come to place their claim on the throne of England.

However, the Godwinesons, a powerful Anglo-Saxon family, believed themselves to be the rightful rulers. The witan, England's ruling council, declared Harold Godwineson (c. 1022–1066) king, but Harold would rule for less than a year.

The Norman Invasion

Harold knew that the Normans were coming, but when the invasion had not occurred by the early fall of 1066, he sent his army home. Then he learned that another Harold, king of Norway, was attempting to invade from the north. On September 25, the two armies met at Stamford Bridge in Yorkshire, and though the English won, the battle exhausted them. Taking advantage of this opportunity, William landed his army in southern England on September 28, and the next day took the town of Hastings.

The English and Normans fought at Hastings on October 14, and though Harold's army put up a good fight, it was no match for the seven thousand Norman warriors. Harold himself died in battle, and now England belonged to William, who received the English crown on Christmas Day.

Norman rule in England

As he had done earlier in Normandy, William spent the coming years securing his power, and in so doing he faced a number of foes—including his son Robert and his brother Odo. Robert had a powerful ally in King Philip I of France, who hoped to gain control of Normandy, and though William gained the victory over all his foes (he sent Robert away, and had Odo imprisoned), the conflicts forced him to devote much of his reign to warfare.

William also instituted a number of reforms designed to strengthen his hold on the throne. Going against the principles of feudalism, which spread power among many nobles, he concentrated as much wealth and authority as he could in the hands of the king. As part of this process, in 1082 he ordered an intensive study of the lands and properties in England, the *Domesday Book*.

Meanwhile, the most lasting effects of the Norman invasion began to work their way into English culture. Norman architecture would prove highly influential on English buildings for centuries to come, but even more important was the Norman effect on the English language. The French-speaking Normans brought a whole new vocabulary to England, whose language was closely related to German. As a result, English today has an amazing array of words, some derived from French and Latin, others from German.

A sad death

In spite of his greatness as a leader, William's latter years were sad ones. He grew extraordinarily fat, so much so that on a military campaign in the summer of 1087, he injured his stomach on his pommel, or saddlehorn. The wound led to an illness from which he would not recover.

Matilda had died in 1083, and when William died on September 9, 1087, he was alone. He had exiled Robert, his eldest son, for his rebellion. William Rufus, his second son and designated heir, was also away, protecting the throne against any challenges from others. (As William II, he would reign from 1087 to 1100.) Finally, William's last surviving son, Henry, destined to reign as Henry I (ruled 1100–35), was busy supervising the collection of his inheritance money.

The aftermath of William's death was as pathetic as the circumstances surrounding it. His body had become so bloated that the pallbearers had a hard time fitting it into the

A scene from the Bayeux Tapestry depicting the English fleeing the Battle of Hastings. William's Norman army was victorious, and William became the king of England. *Reproduced by permission of the Corbis Corporation.*

tomb, and in the struggle to wedge it in, the corpse burst open. The smell of William's decomposing body filled the church, an inglorious end to an otherwise glorious career.

For More Information

Books

Finn, R. Welldon. *An Introduction to Domesday Book.* Westport, CT: Greenwood Press, 1986.

Gormley, Kathleen and Richard Neill. *The Norman Impact on the Medieval World.* New York: Cambridge University Press, 1997.

Green, Robert. *William the Conqueror.* New York: Franklin Watts, 1998.

Martell, Hazel Mary. *The Normans.* New York: New Discovery Books, 1992.

May, Robin. *William the Conqueror and the Normans.* Illustrations by Gerry Wood. New York: Bookwright Press, 1985.

Rickard, Graham. *Norman Castles.* Illustrations by Michael Bragg. New York: Bookwright Press, 1990.

Web Sites

"HWC, William the Conqueror." [Online] Available http://history.idbsu.edu/westciv/willconq/ (last accessed July 26, 2000).

"The Terrible Death of William the Conqueror." *Suite 101.com.* [Online] Available http://www.suite101.com/article.cfm/british_royal_history/15546 (last accessed July 26, 2000).

"William I." *The British Monarchy.* [Online] Available http://www.royal.gov.uk/history/william1.htm (last accessed July 26, 2000).

"William the Conqueror." [Online] Available http://www.geocities.com/Athens/4818/William.htm (last accessed July 26, 2000).

Wu Ze-tian

Born 625
Died 705

Chinese empress

In China as in many other countries, women have exerted an influence over the government without actually holding office. Usually they have been wives or lovers of men in power, and often they have held greater authority than their men. But in nearly four thousand years of Chinese history, only one woman has ever officially ruled China: Wu Ze-tian. During her reign, she proved herself the equal of any man—both in ability and in ruthlessness.

Friends in high places

She is sometimes known as Wu Chao (ZHOW), the name she would take when she assumed the Chinese throne, but she was born Wu Ze-tian or Wu Tse-t'ien (zeh-CHEE-en). Her father, Wu Shi-huo (zhee-WOH), was a wealthy business-man in southeastern China in 617 when he received an im-portant request from Li Yüan (yee-WAHN), then the military commander of the region. At that time, the harsh Sui (SWEE) dynasty ruled China, but Li Yüan had plans for its overthrow, and he needed Wu Shi-huo's help.

"A sage mother will befall and her imperium [empire] will be prosperous forever."

"Prophecy" concerning Wu Ze-tian's rule

In the following year, Li Yüan and his son Li Shih-min (ZHUR-min) took power with the assistance of Wu Shi-huo and others, establishing the T'ang (TAHNG) dynasty. The new emperor rewarded his ally by giving him an important position in the government, and by offering him the cousin of the last Sui emperor, Lady Yang, as his wife. The couple had three daughters, of whom Wu Ze-tian was the second.

Wu Ze-tian was a beautiful young woman, and when Li Shih-min (who had become emperor) heard about her, he arranged for the fourteen-year-old girl to come to the palace. In China, rulers were assigned titles after their death; Li Shih-min is better known to history as **T'ai Tsung** (dy-DZAWNG; see entry), the greatest ruler of T'ang China. Twenty-six years older than Wu Ze-tian, he made her his concubine, a woman whose role toward her "husband" is like that of a wife, but without the social and legal status of a wife.

Jockeying for power

T'ai Tsung became ill in 649, and died later that year. His son and designated successor, Li Chih or Kao Tsung (gow-DZÜNG; ruled 649–83) soon took the throne. As a symbol of mourning, Wu Ze-tian shaved her head and entered a Buddhist temple as a nun; yet she had already attracted the attention of Kao Tsung. He married, but soon afterward, he visited the temple where Wu Ze-tian was living, and asked her to come back to the palace.

Back at the court in 651, twenty-eight-year-old Wu Ze-tian began to exhibit the cleverness and cunning that would make her the most powerful woman in China. She worked to create a friendly relationship with the empress while building a network of spies. The fact that the emperor was madly in love with her, and that the empress had been unable to produce a child, worked in her favor; then in 654, Wu Ze-tian herself presented the emperor with a daughter.

The Chinese valued sons over daughters, and therefore the birth of a girl was not as great a cause for joy as that of a boy—but that hardly explains what Wu Ze-tian did next. Knowing that the emperor adored their daughter, Wu Ze-tian secretly strangled the baby girl; then her spies informed the

Fredegund

Though she never ruled her country as Wu Ze-tian did, the Frankish queen Fredegund (c. 550–597; ruled 561–584) exhibited some of the same ability to achieve and maintain power. Like Wu Ze-tian, she had nerves of steel, and rarely shied away from any act that she deemed necessary to further her own position.

Fredegund first came to the palace of Chilperic (KIL-pur-ik), grandson of **Clovis** (see entry), as a slave girl. Like Wu Ze-tian, however, her beauty soon won her the king's attention. In so doing, she displaced the queen, Audovera, who had borne Chilperic three sons, but Fredegund remained a concubine and not a full-fledged wife.

In 567, Chilperic took a second wife, Galswintha; but Galswintha was strangled in her bed soon after the wedding. It is not clear whether Fredegund arranged her murder, but in any case she now had no serious competition for the king's affection.

In the years that followed, Fredegund proved herself more vicious than Chilperic in dealing with his enemies, and she ordered numerous assassinations. Meanwhile, she tried to increase her own standing at court by producing a son and heir to her husband. At least then she would stand a chance that her offspring could become ruler while she wielded the real power behind the throne. Several efforts failed, however, and two of her boys died in childhood. But several of Audovera's sons died too, and Fredegund finally succeeded in murdering Audovera and the latter's last remaining son.

Fredegund left a trail of bodies behind her, a death toll that is too long to recount. One of her favorite tactics was to use one person to help her get rid of another, then murder her former ally as well. In fact she may have been responsible for her own husband's death—but not before she bore a son, Chlothar (KLOH-thar), who lived. Chlothar finally took power in 596, but Fredegund had little opportunity to enjoy her success: she died a year later.

emperor that the empress was responsible. This gave Kao Tsung an excuse to set the empress aside, and Wu Ze-tian took her place as his number-one wife. The former empress died soon afterward, most likely through the efforts of Wu Ze-tian.

Quarrels with her sons

Kao Tsung became increasingly ill, and as his power faded, that of Wu Ze-tian grew. She became involved in making policy and proved herself an able leader, introducing a twelve-point program of reform that included reductions in the military, taxes, and forced labor; increases of salaries for government officials; and improvements in agricultural production. These measures won her a great deal of support.

In 674, Wu Ze-tian created the titles of Heavenly Emperor and Heavenly Empress for her husband and herself. By this point, she and the emperor had three sons, but the first one died mysteriously, probably murdered by his mother. Then in 680, the second son was charged with starting a rebellion, and he was sent away.

Three years later, Kao Tsung died, and the third son, Li Che, took the throne. He proved incapable as a ruler, and shortly afterward Wu Ze-tian replaced him with a fourth son, Li Tan. Her tampering had made Wu Ze-tian a number of enemies, and in 686 they launched an armed rebellion against her. She managed to put down this uprising, along with a second one several years later.

Sole ruler of China

With Li Tan still on the throne, Wu Ze-tian set about consolidating her power. This she did in part by giving help to poor people around the country and by punishing corrupt officials. She was further assisted by a couple of items that were mysteriously discovered around the same time. One was a white stone bearing the words "A sage mother will befall and her imperium will be prosperous forever." This, along with a Buddhist scripture that predicted the coming of a great female ruler, were interpreted as prophecies of Wu Ze-tian's reign. These "prophecies" certainly appeared at a convenient time for Wu Ze-tian, and it is likely she arranged to have them planted and discovered.

In 690, she received three petitions, one signed by more than sixty thousand people, asking her to take power. Using this as justification, she removed Li Tan from power, and declared the end of the T'ang dynasty. Wu Ze-tian, now sixty-six years old, assumed the throne under the Zhou (ZHOH) dynasty, though as it turned out, she would be the only ruler in this dynasty.

Over the fifteen years of her reign, Wu Ze-tian once again proved herself an able administrator. She promoted men of talent and honesty, and her troops won a number of victories. But in 705, when she was eighty-one years old, one of her officials led a rebellion against her, and Wu Ze-tian realized that she was too old to maintain power. When the official restored the throne to Li Che (who was then replaced in 710 by Li Tan), she put up no fight. She died in November 705.

For More Information

Books

Ashby, Ruth and Deborah Gore Ohrn, editors. *Herstory: Women Who Changed the World*. Introduction by Gloria Steinem. New York: Viking, 1995.

Asimov, Isaac. *The Dark Ages*. Boston: Houghton Mifflin, 1968.

Chiang, Ch'eng-an. *Empress of China, Wu Ze Tian*. Monterey, CA: Victory Press, 1998.

Reese, Lyn. *The Eyes of the Empress: Women in Tang Dynasty China*. Berkeley, CA: Women in World History, 1996.

Web Sites

"Ancient China: The T'ang, 618–970." [Online] Available http://www.wsu.edu:8080/~dee/CHEMPIRE/TANG.HTM (last accessed July 26, 2000).

"Female Heroes: Empress Wu Zetian." *Women in World History*. [Online] Available http://www.womeninworldhistory.com/heroine6.html (last accessed July 26, 2000).

"The Franks." [Online] Available http://www.btinternet.com/~mark.furnival/franks.htm (last accessed July 26, 2000).

"Fredegund." *Imperium*. [Online] Available http://www.ghgcorp.com/shetler/oldimp/147.html (last accessed July 26, 2000).

"The T'ang Dynasty (A.D. 618–907)." [Online] Available http://deall.ohio-state.edu/jin.3/c231/handouts/h9.htm (last accessed July 26, 2000).

Index

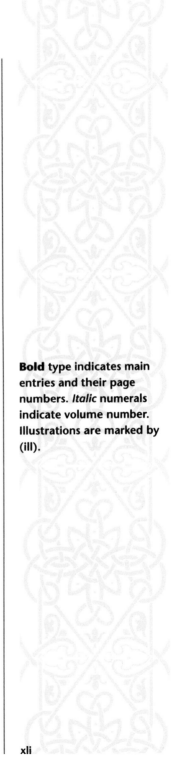

Bold type indicates main entries and their page numbers. *Italic* numerals indicate volume number. Illustrations are marked by (ill).

114, 133, 146, 169–71, 185, 187, 189, *2:* 204, 246, 274

Charles Martel *1:* 62

Charles the Bold *2:* 246–47, 247 (ill.)

Charles V *1:* 69, 70, 73

Charles VI *1:* 73

Charles VII *2:* 191, 193

Chatillon *2:* 326

Chaucer, Geoffrey *1:* 59, 113, **118–19,** 118 (ill.), *2:* 267

Cheng Ho *1:* 156, 159, *2:* 220, 339

Childeric *1:* 78

Children's Crusade *1:* 182

Chilperic *1:* 79, *2:* 373

China *1:* 4, 56, 129, 134, 156, 157, 159, 161, 164, 165, 188, 190, *2:* 209–15, 220, 267, 298–301, 303, 304, 329–32, 335–42, 347, 357–62, 371, 372, 374, 375

Ch'in Shih Huang Ti *2:* 361

Chlodomir *1:* 79, 83

Chlothar *2:* 373

Chola *1:* 10, 14

Chou *2:* 357, 358

Christ. *See* Jesus Christ

Christendom *1:* 37, 47, 142, 181

Christianity *1:* 1, 23–29, 35, 36, 51, 58, 62, 79–81, 86–88, 114, 124, 126, 139, 141, 142, 145, 158, 175, 187, *2:* 204, 205, 212, 213, 218, 258, 260, 261, 263, 274, 276, 290, 291–94, 305, 316, 324, 326, 328, 340, 351, 352, 361

Christianization *1:* 44

Christine de Pisan *1:* **69–75,** 69 (ill.)

Christmas *1:* 18, 65, *2:* 267, 292, 368

Chronographia 2: 353

Church and state *1:* 115, 145, 150, 151

Church of San Vitale *1:* 64, *2:* 202–04

Church of St. John Lateran *1:* 125

Church of St. Julian *2:* 309

Church of the Holy Apostles *2:* 205

Chu Ti *2:* 339

Chu Yüan-chang *2:* 339

Cilicia *2:* 298

Cistercian Order *1:* 47, 48, 52, *2:* 311

City of God 1: 23, 28, 29, 74

City of Ladies, The 1: 69, 73, 74

City-state *1:* 15, *2:* 297

Clare of Assisi *1:* 125

Clement II (pope) *1:* 146

Clement III (antipope) *1:* 150, 151

Clement III (pope) *1:* 173, 179

Clement IV (pope) *2:* 241

Clotilde *1:* 77, 77 (ill.), 79, 80

Clovis *1:* 61, 62, **77–83,** 77 (ill.), *2:* 329, 373

Cluny *1:* 180

Code of Maimonides 2: 225

Coleridge, Samuel Taylor *2:* 214 (ill.), 215

Cologne *1:* 80, *2:* 351

Columbus, Christopher *2:* 217, 304

Communion *1:* 85

Communism *1:* 18, *2:* 274

Comnena, Anna. *See* Anna Comnena

Comnenus, Alexis I. *See* Alexis I Comnenus

Compiègne *1:* 2

Concerning Famous Women 1: 74

Concordat of Worms *1:* 115, 151

Confessions (Augustine) *1:* 23, 24, 28

Confessions (St. Patrick) *2:* 289, 290, 294, 295

Confucianism *1:* 4, *2:* 329, 331, 336

Confucius *1:* 165, *2:* 331, 359

Conrad III *1:* 172

Conrad of Montferrat *2:* 316

Consolation of Philosophy 1: 53, 57, 59

Constantine (Roman emperor) *2:* 293

Constantine V *1:* 186

Constantine VI *1:* 186, 187, 188

Constantinople *1:* 86–89, 137, 138, 140, 158, 166, 167, 182, 186, 187, *2:* 199–201, 204, 205, 273, 275–78, 301, 353, 360. *See also* Istanbul

Copernicus, Nicolaus *2:* 237

Córdoba *1:* 31, 34, 35, *2:* 224

Z